MAR DEL

NORT

Tropicus Cancri

La Bermuda

ESPANOLA

Millaria Germanica
Leuca Hispanica

Amstelodami, Apud Ioannem Ianssonium

THE QUEST FOR CAPTAIN MORGAN

Sir Henry Morgan

John Ure

THE QUEST FOR CAPTAIN MORGAN

Constable London

First published in Great Britain 1983
by Constable & Company Ltd
10 Orange Street London WC2H 7EG
Copyright © 1983 by John Ure
ISBN 0 09 465260 0
Set in Linotron Plantin 11 pt by
Rowland Phototypesetting Ltd
Bury St Edmunds, Suffolk
Printed in Great Britain by
St Edmundsbury Press
Bury St Edmunds, Suffolk

Dedicated
with gratitude and respect
but without formal permission
to
ST CHRISTOPHER
but for whose active intervention
in the Sierra de Escambray
on the 7th of October 1980
this book and its author
would have been prematurely terminated

Contents

Illustrations

Except where otherwise stated, all photographs are by
Caroline Ure or the author.

Acknowledgements

This book describes both Captain Morgan's Caribbean exploits and my own attempts to retrace these on the ground – and in some cases on the water. In the course of compiling the material for it, I have therefore become indebted to two separate groups of people.

Firstly, I am grateful to those who directed me towards useful source material about Morgan. In Cuba, Dr Eusebio Leal (director of the *Museo Historico de la Habana*) and Dr Gustavo Sed (official historian of the Province of Camaguey) were most co-operative; in Jamaica, Mr Clinton Black (keeper of the official archives) and Dr David Buisseret (of the University of the West Indies) entered into the spirit of my enterprise; in England, Mr Rohan Butler (of All Souls' College, Oxford), Miss Kate Crowe (of the Historical Section of the Foreign and Commonwealth Office), Dr M. W. B. Sanderson (of the National Maritime Museum) and Dr Helen Wallis (Map Librarian of the British Library) all pointed me in some useful directions, and the staff of the Library and Map Room of the Royal Geographical Society were most patient in assisting me. I am also especially indebted to the authors of two admirable modern biographies of Morgan – Mr Dudley Pope and Mr Peter Earle – whose own researches have provided signposts for later comers; their books are referred to in my text and listed in the bibliography.

Secondly, I am grateful to those who have helped me on my travels. Notable among them have been Captain Jorge Fernandez (Cuban Minister of Fisheries), Sr Julio Imperatori (Vice-President of the National Bank of Cuba), Mr John Drinkall (formerly British High Commissioner at Kingston), Mr John

Sanders (formerly HM Ambassador at Panama City), and Major A. Dutton (honorary British consul at Merida in Mexico) whose particular kindnesses are described in my narrative. Numerous others played a role in our travels and it has seemed diplomatic to describe some of them with their names and identities disguised. We shall remember them all with affection.

Finally, as always, I am grateful to my wife Caroline, not only for many of the photographs which illustrate this book but also for accompanying me on all the journeys involved in retracing Captain Morgan's exploits except those – involving nights on Cuban fishing boats or in camp with US Rangers – where her presence would have disconcerted others more than it encouraged me. In Latin America respect for the proprieties can still be a more potent restraint than apprehension of danger or discomfort.

Prologue: a Theory and an Idea

Even in the worst moments of wading through mangrove swamp, and in the best moments of sailing between the coral reefs, I could always remember how the project had started. It had not been a big night at the Beefsteak Club; only some half dozen members had pressed the bell in the shady entrance off London's Leicester Square, given their names to the steward over the house telephone, climbed the steep stairs and found themselves in the long, high chamber – resembling a Nonconformist chapel – which constituted the dining-room, smoking-room, coffee-room and indeed all the other public rooms of the club rolled into one. They had paused at the hatch into the steward's office, studied the evening's menu and ordered their meal. Then they had walked past the long dining-table, seeing themselves reflected in the highly polished silver, and asked Charles to bring them a drink.

Charles was not really the man's name, but all the club servants were addressed by members as 'Charles'; it was one of the club's many idiosyncrasies, and saved the members the effort of thought without appearing to cause any crises of identity to the stewards. Charles called the members to the table one by one as their meals emerged from the kitchen. Obediently they took their places in the order of their calling: the first at the right of the head of the table, the second at the left, the third – even if he were the youngest or newest member – at the head.

If members of the Beefsteak are feeling sulky or silent or shy they do not come to the club, because it is one of the unwritten rules that members talk to their neighbours at meals as they would at a private dinner party. On this occasion, a celebrated art historian was arguing with an Oxford philosopher about how the Roman cavalry had managed without stirrups; a former Conservative cabinet minister was discussing with a fashionable QC the circumstances in which mutiny at sea could be justified; and a member of the College of Heralds was informing a knight of the theatre that he thought the Order of the Garter owed its origin to a much more intimate object than a garter having been dropped on that medieval dance floor. Charles brought the port and the Stilton. Gradually the conversation became general.

It was the actor who put forward the fatal theory, in reply to something the QC had said.

'All countries grow their souls in a particular moment of their history. The Italians have a Cinquecento soul. The English are all Elizabethans at heart: Drake and Shakespeare and Tudor cottages . . . that's what we're all about. The Americans came of spiritual age with the opening up of the West in the last century: Custer's last stand was their confirmation day. Now take Russia . . . take Russia . . .'

There was a pause as we all took Russia.

'The Russians still have a nineteenth-century soul. They are all really characters out of Dostoevsky if they live in cities, and out of Turgenev or Chekhov if they live in the country. Railway stations are their spiritual shrines. Given half a chance they'd turn a spacecraft into a Victorian parlour just as we'd turn one into a mock-Tudor cabin.'

'Perhaps,' said the Oxford don, 'the key to understanding a country is to fathom its essential period and relate its present state to that.'

Further down the table, a retired merchant-navy captain who was the actor's guest ('presumably because he wants to study a rolling gait for his next part' one uncharitable member had commented) was becoming somewhat restive at the turn the conversation had taken.

'Countries growing souls! What a crackpot notion! Now if they were to grow characteristic *bodies*, that really might give you something to talk about. I can see it all' – a glint came into his sharp though bloodshot eye: 'Germany, all bosoms and bottoms like one of those full-blown opera singers; Switzerland, all tucked up as prim as a spinster's counterpane; Egypt, all groping fingers and hot armpits . . .'

'You paint a very pretty pageant,' commented the art historian dryly, 'but – to go back to what we were saying – a country's essential period is not just a question of pictures or architecture. It's what makes people tick. Find their period: build on that. If I were a diplomat' – he turned towards me – 'I'd decide first when I went to a new country what its essential period was, when its soul was born if you like, and then I'd delve into that. But I hear you're off to somewhere: where is it?'

'I'm off to the Caribbean,' I said.

'The Caribbean!' The famous actor's face took on an expression that had compelled the attention of a thousand audiences. 'A clear case of a seventeenth-century soul if ever I saw one! Buccaneers and brigantines, rum and coral islands, mutinies and treasure hunts . . . why, they're still at it . . . hijackers and yachts, daiquiris and scuba fishing, coups and hashish-running . . . nothing but the names have changed. Take my word for it, you should write a book about the seventeenth century if you want to get close to the Caribbean.'

'But I don't write books about centuries,' I protested. 'I write books about people, or about journeys, or about people making journeys.'

'Then you must find a seventeenth-century character who lived in the Caribbean. It shouldn't be too difficult. What about Penn, or Venables, who captured Jamaica? Or Sir Walter Raleigh's expedition up the Orinoco in 1618? Or those buccaneering exploits by Morgan or one of his gang of cutthroats?'

'I don't much like the idea of any of them,' I said. 'Penn and Venables captured Jamaica almost by accident. Raleigh isn't really a seventeenth-century figure – he's an Elizabethan. And surely Sir Henry Morgan was a pretty unappealing character – diabolically cruel to his prisoners, double-crossing to his shipmates, a pirate who turned King's evidence . . . I'm not sure I should want to write a book about *him*.'

The name of Morgan rang a bell in what was clearly becoming

the progressively more clouded mind of the master mariner down the table.

'*Captain* Morgan – that the Morgan you mean? They named a rum after him, you know. Damned good drink – blend of Jamaican, Barbadian and some other pretty potent hooches. Damn clever publicity for it too; used to see ads all over Southampton saying "when did you last have some yo-ho-ho?" or something like that . . . pretty girl in the ad too, looked as if . . .'

His sentence, like his line of thought, trailed off into ever less coherent recollections, doubtless of a yo-ho-ho variety, and in the absence of more evocative hooch he helped himself to another glass of vintage port.

'I think you've been reading the wrong books about Morgan,' said the Oxford don to me. 'Can't blame you. Some of his own crew started libelling him in his lifetime and the habit stuck. Most of the stuff written about him make him out to be as bad as Bluebeard. But even if he was a bit rough and ready, he was a fine combined-operations commander – the first, you might say.'

'I'll think about Morgan,' I promised, and the conversation moved on to the ethics of interrogating prisoners of war; it was punctuated periodically by yo-ho-ho-ish remarks from down the table about all the intelligence that might have been picked up by the Allies in the Burma campaign 'if only those young pink-faced public-school boys hadn't been so squeamish about taking a grip of Nip POWs by the short and curly.'

And think about Morgan I did. The first thing I discovered about him, when I started my researches, was that he had really made the Caribbean his oyster. As a mere boy he had taken part in the capture of Jamaica for the British Crown, or rather for the English Commonwealth of Cromwell. As a young man he had taken part in buccaneering raids on the Mexican coast and on Cuba. As an independent commander, and later with the resounding title of Admiral of the Brethren of the Coast, he had led raids on Cuba again, on the Gulf of Maracaibo in Venezuela and twice on the Isthmus of Panama. Morgan had not made just one journey in the Caribbean: he had made a whole series of journeys on land and sea, any one of which it would be an exciting challenge to retrace. And all the time he had not only been sailing close to the wind in the tricky reef-infested waters of the Caribbean, but he had also been sailing close to the wind in the even trickier political waters of Charles II's England.

Morgan's raids – like those of Drake and Raleigh before him – were made on the Spanish Main at a time when England was more often than not at peace with Spain. Yet Morgan was not – in the strict sense – a pirate. He was a privateer, carrying a commission from the Governor of Jamaica. Where Morgan ran into trouble was when his privateering activities went beyond the limited objective of frustrating Spanish invasion attempts on Jamaica, or when he committed some particularly audacious raid – such as that on the city of Panama – after a peace treaty had been signed but before his privateer's commission had been withdrawn. Had he wilfully ravaged a Spanish city in time of peace, or had he genuinely not known that a treaty had been signed?

It was to find the answer to this question (or at least to persuade the Spanish ambassador that he was trying to find the answer to this question) that Charles II had had Morgan brought back from Jamaica to London as a state prisoner. It took Morgan three years to clear himself, but clear himself he did, to such good effect that the King knighted him and sent him back as lieutenant-governor of Jamaica. Now it was his job to restrain those buccaneers who had formerly been his companions from acts of piracy or excessive privateering.

The career about which I began to read was not only one which would take me into every corner of the Caribbean, it was also one which would take me along the broad highways and into the tortuous byways of seventeenth-century history. Here was a man whose public career touched upon the founding of the first English colony, upon the use of sea power in the New World, upon the ethics of buccaneering, upon the economics of sugar plantations and the slave trade; and whose private career was a swashbuckling rampage through bottles of rum and chests of pieces-of-eight! If it were true that the Caribbean had a

seventeenth-century soul, then surely here was the embodi-
ment of that soul.

My destination as a diplomat was Cuba. It was here, in its
seaport capital of Havana, that I expected to be based for the
next couple of years. Apart from Jamaica itself, there could
hardly be a better jumping-off place for retracing Morgan's
exploits. From my office window I looked out over the Morro
Castle guarding the entrance to Havana harbour. Morgan had
seen this very view from his flagship in 1668 and had concluded
– almost for the only time in his life – that discretion was the
better part of valour: he had selected a softer target on the
southern side of Cuba. I would go there, and to all the other
scenes of his exploits.

But first I needed to get a clearer idea of the structure of the
Caribbean in the mid-seventeenth century when the young
Henry Morgan arrived there. How firmly was the Spanish
empire established? Where were its main bastions? How and
where was the fabled treasure collected from the mines of Peru
and the hinterland of Mexico? Where and why had the buccaneers come into existence? It seemed essential to find answers
to all these and many other questions before I could understand
why Morgan had gone where he went and done what he did. My
first voyage must be a voyage of academic discovery, and my
first march a march backwards in time.

Life Beyond the Line: the Heroic Period

When Henry Morgan first caught sight of the West Indies in 1655 it was already 163 years since Columbus had discovered them, and the Spanish had dominated the region for the whole of that time.

The cardinal principle of their domination had been its exclusivity. Almost the first act of the Spanish king on learning of the existence of the New World was to send hot-foot to the Vatican to persuade Pope Alexander VI to cede sovereignty over the territories discovered, and – more significantly – over those to be discovered, to the Spanish crown. This the Pope – mindful no doubt of his indebtedness to Ferdinand and Isabella of Spain for earlier support – promptly did: by the papal bull *Inter Caetera* of 3 May 1493, Spain was not only granted dominion over the newly discovered region in perpetuity, but the Pope warned off 'by the authority of Almighty God . . . all persons, no matter their rank, estate, degree, order or condition from daring, without your special permission, to go for the purpose of trading or for any other purpose whatever, to the said islands and countries after they have been discovered and found by your envoys or other persons sent out by you for that purpose.' The western hemisphere was to be a *chasse gardée*, even if for the moment it was not recognized as a western hemisphere but still thought of as the off-shore islands of Marco Polo's China.

The Portuguese were not long in persuading the Pope to modify his bull, to bring it into line with earlier concessions made to them. His Holiness declared that all lands on the European side of a line one hundred leagues (three hundred miles) west of the Azores should remain the fief of Portugal, and

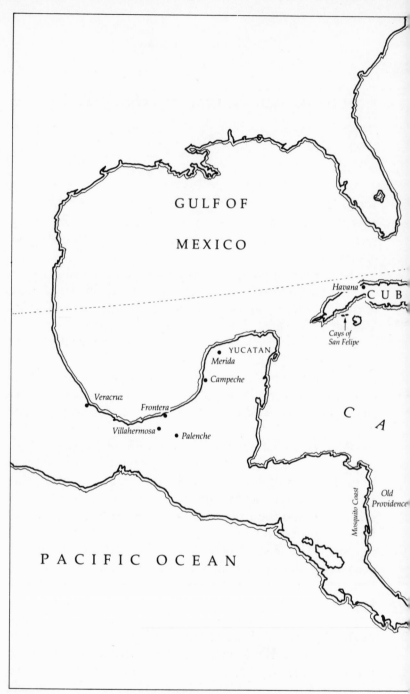

GULF OF

MEXICO

Havana ● C U B

Cays of
San Felipe

YUCATAN ●
Merida ●
Campeche ●

Veracruz ●
Frontera ●
Villahermosa ● ● Palenche

C   A

Mosquito Coast
Old
Providence

PACIFIC OCEAN

Map of the Caribbean

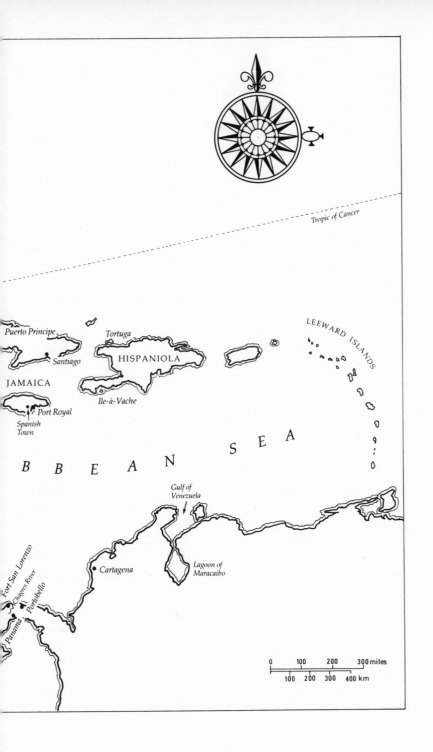

Tropic of Cancer

Puerto Principe

Tortuga

LEEWARD ISLANDS

Santiago

HISPANIOLA

JAMAICA

Ile-à-Vache

Port Royal

Spanish
Town

B   B   E   A   N   S   E   A

Gulf of
Venezuela

B   B   E   A   N

Fort San Lorenzo

Chagres River

Cartagena

Lagoon of
Maracaibo

Portobello

Panama

0   100   200   300 miles

100   200   300   400 km

all land discovered further than that limit – 'beyond the Line' – should belong to Spain. This arbitrary division was later modified, and further sanctified in the eyes of the participants, by the Treaty of Tordesillas in 1494.* It followed from this that all those who sailed beyond the Line, be they Englishmen, Frenchmen or Dutchmen, be they explorers, traders or naval commanders, were considered by the Spaniards as trespassers and potential pirates. The normal code of honour (so precious to the Spaniards) was not deemed relevant in dealing with such intruders, as Sir John Hawkins discovered at Veracruz in 1568 when the Spaniards attacked him after negotiating a truce. The normal code of treatment of prisoners (observed – by and large – in European continental wars) was not deemed appropriate for heretics caught defying the Pope's edicts, as countless English seamen learnt at the hands of the Inquisition or in the dungeons or salt mines of the New World. The normal cessation of hostilities following peace treaties between European powers was not deemed to extend to the Caribbean, where the prevailing sentiment was 'no peace beyond the Line.'

If exclusivity was the first principle of Spanish colonial development in the New World, the second principle was concentration on extraction of wealth. The Spaniards who landed on the Caribbean islands or on the mainland of central or south America were not interested in sugar or tobacco plantations, in cattle ranches or timber forests; they came looking solely for precious metals. After Cortes had captured Aztec temples lined with sheets of gold, and after Pizarro had uncovered the treasures of the Incas and discovered the mines of Potosí whence these treasures came, all efforts were concentrated on maximizing the flow of bullion back to metropolitan Spain. Records kept by the Spanish Council of the Indies indicate how successful these efforts were. In the course of the sixteenth century alone, Spain sent back from her possessions in the New World three times as much gold and silver as had been in circulation in Europe at the beginning of that century.

---

* See the author's *Prince Henry the Navigator* (London, 1977), page 188.

Not only did the kings of Spain – notably Philip II – not consider developing agriculture and other industries in the new colonies, they allowed agriculture and industry to wither in metropolitan Spain itself: with such huge injections of bullion into the economy, conventional labour seemed superfluous.

But one activity in Spain and her colonies which did not seem superfluous to the Spanish monarchy was administration. Meticulous control was the third guiding principle of Spain in relation to her overseas possessions. With so much wealth accruing from looting and mining in such distant territories, the scope for peculation was immense. Philip II and his successors therefore decided that every stage of the journey from the gold mines of Mexico and the silver mines of Peru to the royal treasuries in Seville and Madrid should be prescribed, scheduled, supervised and recorded. Those who might otherwise have been employed in farming or manufacturing were set to work as lading clerks and tax collectors, as storekeepers and inspectors. Of the six million inhabitants of Spain in the early seventeenth century, a totally disproportionate number – estimates vary, but all run into many hundreds of thousands – worked in the administration either of the State or of the ubiquitous Church. The system which all this administration set up was complex and fascinating in itself; it also provided the temptations and opportunities which were to be so lucratively exploited by Sir Henry Morgan and the buccaneers of the seventeenth century.

In its most simple outline, this was how it worked. There were two main areas in which gold or silver was found or mined by the Spaniards: one was the interior of New Spain (Mexico), and the other was the interior of Peru (which included those regions now also forming Bolivia and Ecuador). Mule trains brought the Mexican bullion to the port of Veracruz. That from Peru and the west coast of South America had a more arduous initial journey. It was first transported in small ships up the Pacific coast to old Panama City. From Panama it had to cross the isthmus from Pacific to Caribbean ports. The crossing was made on mules, on ponies, or on flat-bottomed boats up the

Chagres river; both mule tracks and river ran through the dense jungle terrain of the isthmus. Originally, Nombre de Dios was the terminal of the crossing, then Fort Lorenzo at the mouth of the Chagres river, then Portobello forty miles further east. Nombre de Dios and Fort Lorenzo had no proper anchorages for the galleons, so the treasure had to be shipped onward yet again in small coastal vessels – this time through the Caribbean – to Cartagena, the impregnable Spanish stronghold on the northern coast of what is now Colombia. A fleet of Spanish galleons then picked up the bullion from Cartagena or Portobello and carried it, not directly back to Spain, but to Havana in Cuba. There the galleons joined the other fleet of Spanish ocean-going cargo ships – known colloquially as the *flota* – which had come with the Mexican gold from Veracruz. Galleons and *flota* then proceeded across the Atlantic in convoy to Sanlucar de Barrameda (the port for Seville) where they had to brave the sand-bar across the mouth of the Guadalquivir river before finally depositing their rich cargo in the vaults of the king's treasure house at Seville.

The whole journey was fraught with hazards. The mule trains across the isthmus of Panama could be ambushed, as they had been by Drake in 1573. Or the small ships plying between Nombre de Dios and Cartagena could be sunk by 'northers' – squalls from the Caribbean. Either the galleons, or the *flota*, or both, could be attacked at sea on their way to Havana, as the former had been by Jean d'Argo in 1556. Havana itself could be attacked and sacked, as it had been by François le Clerc's men in 1553. Lastly the joint convoys, even with a heavy escort of Spanish warships, could be waylaid off the Azores on their approaches to Europe, as they were by Seigneur de Dolhain's Protestant privateers in the 1580s, or as they were again at Tenerife by Admiral Blake in 1657. It was a wonder that as much bullion reached the royal coffers as it did.

With such a dangerous journey facing his treasure, it might have been imagined that King Philip II and his successors would have done everything possible to protect it. They did not. Instead, they were obsessed by the need for orderly administration. The movements of the galleons and the *flota* were dictated not by considerations of wind and weather, but by considerations of meeting interest payments due to the Spanish royal bankers, or paying the troops campaigning in the cause of the Spanish royal ambitions in the Low Countries. Nautical and security factors were at all points subordinated to economic or political ones.

It would have been a tempting situation even if the Caribbean had remained a Spanish private lake. But it had not. In the years between Columbus and Morgan, the Spanish dominion over the New World had been challenged and found to be precarious.

The first intruders beyond the Line had – in many cases – not intended any challenge. They had mostly been trading vessels genuinely interested in buying the goods for which the West Indies were becoming famous: hides, dyes, timber and so on. It was all the easier to pursue profitable commerce because the Spanish settlers were anxious to buy. Their own supply vessels came rarely; the galleons brought provisions, and the goods they carried were unnecessarily expensive because they were subject to heavy duties imposed by the Spanish Crown. Many earlier adventurers into the New World – Sir John Hawkins among them – would have been content enough if they could have traded and smuggled their way to wealth. But the Spanish Crown would have none of it: all foreign ships were pirate ships and were to be treated accordingly. It was little wonder that even those who might have had more mundane intentions were soon forced into fighting for their profits, and found raiding more lucrative than trading.

By the beginning of the seventeenth century, another class of foreigner was also intruding on the Spanish preserve: settlers were arriving. Thomas Warner started planting tobacco in St Kitts in 1623. John Powell brought English settlers to Barbados a few months later. English colonisers moved on from St Kitts to Nevis in 1628 and to Antigua in 1632. French settlers followed the English, and the Dutch occupied the islands of Curaçao, Bonaire and Aruba further south and immediately off the Spanish Main. Soon sugar and cotton were augmenting tobacco as popular crops.

It might have been thought that these small planters' settlements would not have unduly worried the Spaniards: they were not interfering with the extraction of precious metals. But not only was their mere existence viewed as an affront, it was soon realized that they provided harbours, repair yards and supply bases for the traders and raiders who were operating further west. Worse, they were to windward of the Greater Antilles – Cuba, Jamaica, Hispaniola – and therefore their ships could swoop down suddenly on these vulnerable targets, or on the rich townships of the Spanish Main itself – Portobello, Nombre de Dios, Cartagena. The English colonies were worse than an affront: they were a strategic threat.

The settlers spawned another breed of intruder, neither planter nor merchant, neither privateer nor pirate. These were the *boucaniers*, cast-outs from the embryonic colonies or from their home countries. Many of them were apprentices whose work on the tobacco estates had been taken over by imported African slave labour. Some were Huguenot refugees from Richelieu's France, or Dutch Protestants who had fled from the Spanish Netherlands, or Royalists who had left Cromwell's England. Others were criminals who had been sentenced to deportation, or prisoners of war, or sailors who had mutinied or been marooned. A few were even runaway slaves. These *boucaniers* formed themselves into gangs along the coasts or in the interiors of the Caribbean islands. They lived by killing the wild cattle which had been allowed to run loose. They derived their name from the way they cooked their meat, cutting it into long strips and smoking it over a slow fire, resulting in a product called *boucan*. As the Spanish made life ever more difficult for the *boucaniers* in the Greater Antilles, more and more of them tended to concentrate on the small turtle-shaped island of Tortuga just off the north-west coast of Hispaniola. Cattle hunting was less easy here. The community was ripe for other employment. Adventurous sea captains, intent on despoiling Spanish settlements or shipping, could always pick up a crew here. The *boucaniers* were developing into the buccaneers.

But while the buccaneers were based on Tortuga or other small islands, and while they had no national backing or protection, they were a nuisance rather than a menace to the Spanish imperial design. In 1655 this changed abruptly. In that year for the first time an important island – one of the Greater Antilles themselves – was captured from Spain and passed into the permanent occupation of a semi-permanent enemy: Jamaica fell to the British.

How this far-reaching development came about reflected little credit on anyone. Oliver Cromwell, tiring of Spanish intransigence over the two subjects that preoccupied him in the New World – freedom of worship and freedom of trade – developed his Western Design. He sent a fleet and an army, under the command of Admiral Penn and General Venables respectively, to start the process of seizing the Spanish empire – a task which he was encouraged to think was possible by Thomas Gage (a renegade Catholic priest of which much more will be heard in this book). The initial target was to be the large and centrally situated island of Hispaniola (now divided between the countries of Haiti and the Dominican Republic). The attack was a disastrous fiasco, and it is difficult to decide whether more blame for this attached to Penn or to Venables. Fearing to sail his ships too close to the defences of Santo Domingo, the capital city and immediate object of their assault, Penn and his vice-admiral sailed on down the coast and landed their forces in entirely the wrong places. Venables then led a half-hearted and abortive overland expedition against the city. The Spanish defenders drove the assailants off, and the local dysentery, malaria and dengue fever accounted for what little was left of their spirit and two thousand of their lives. The whole expedition withdrew in disorder and decided to look for a softer target.

Jamaica, though more strategically placed, more defensible and enjoying better harbours, turned out to be an easier proposition. Within a day of the first landings, the capital was in English hands; and within a week the Spanish governor was

A typical buccaneer, with long musket, hunting dogs and clay pipe, as illustrated in the French edition of Esquemeling's history

suing for surrender terms. Penn and Venables hurried back to London to give their own differing excuses and vindications of their failure to take Hispaniola. Cromwell was unimpressed and considered their premature return amounted to desertion; he had them incarcerated in the Tower (though not for long, and Sir William Penn was to feature again in his country's history, not least by fathering the founder of Pennsylvania).

However critical he was of Penn's and Venables's performance, Cromwell did not fail to reinforce and populate Jamaica: common criminals, wayward Irish girls, Scottish vagrants and other misfits in his puritanical Protectorate were dispatched to live there. Almost absent-mindedly, Britain had acquired her first major colony in the West Indies, and Spain had admitted a Trojan horse within her empire.

Acquiring such a possession might be easy: maintaining it was harder. For the first years after the British invasion, there was actually a Spanish resistance force living and fighting in the mountains on the north coast of the island. A small British naval squadron, under the command of Commodore Christopher Mings, was occupied in trying to prevent the Spanish stay-behind forces from receiving supplies and reinforcements from nearby Cuba. But soon it became clear that neither Cromwell nor, when the responsibility became his at the Restoration in 1660, King Charles II could spare a fleet of the strength and size necessary to ensure the long-term security of Jamaica. Indeed, Charles II had contemplated handing back Jamaica to Spain as a *quid pro quo* for Spanish help over the Restoration; but he was prevailed upon not to forgo such a promising prospect of strategic and commercial advantage as that represented by the new-born colony. The young Lord Windsor was dispatched, after a briefing at the Admiralty by Samuel Pepys, to be the new governor; it was made clear to him that it would be no good looking to London for the supply of frigates and soldiers to protect his domain. He would have to rely on local resources.

Fortunately, some local resources were emerging. Commodore Mings had captured a number of Spanish ships plying between Cartagena and Portobello. By 1662, when Lord Windsor arrived, a very substantial number of buccaneers had migrated to Jamaica from Tortuga and elsewhere. Mings handed over his prizes to them and they in turn swelled the forces under his command. Mings's squadron was beginning to look less and less like a unit of the Royal Navy and more and more like a motley bunch of irregulars. Lord Windsor was at last acquiring those 'local resources' on which the King and Mr Pepys had been enjoining him to depend.

In September 1662, only a few weeks after Lord Windsor's arrival in Port Royal, the word went out to the buccaneers there assembled that commissions would be issued to them as privateers to join an expedition being mounted by Mings against the Spanish city of Santiago in Cuba. A retaliatory stroke was to be struck against the port from which Spain had – for the past seven years – been threatening Jamaica; the terms of the contract were the usual ones of 'no purchase, no pay', but there should be rich pickings to be had from so well-established and opulent a city as Santiago. Ten private vessels came forward to join the two which Mings commanded in the King's name. One of the smallest of them was commanded by a young settler and soldier of fortune who had borrowed the money for his share in the ship. His name was Henry Morgan. It was his first appearance in the annals of his country's history.

Henry Morgan had arrived in Jamaica, as a lad of nineteen, with the original invasion force of Penn and Venables. He had been born in Wales, almost certainly at the village of Llanrhymney near Tredegar. He was thought to have been descended from a certain Sir Thomas Morgan, who had distinguished himself fighting the Spaniards in the Low Countries in the reign of Queen Elizabeth I. With considerably more historical evidence, he appears to have been the nephew of two brothers – Edward and Thomas Morgan – who were soldiers of fortune in Germany during the Thirty Years' War and then fought on opposite sides during the English Civil War. Both rose to military positions of distinction on their respective sides, Edward – the Cavalier – probably having the greater influence on the young Henry during the Civil War years since he was

Samuel Pepys who, as Secretary to the Navy, was concerned with the
defence of Jamaica

campaigning with the Royalist forces in Wales. After the war, however, it was probably Thomas – the Roundhead – who was able to use his influence to get his nephew accepted for service with the expedition sent out by Cromwell – under Penn and Venables – to further his Western Design. One thing is certain: the military influence, from one side and then from the other, must have been strong in Henry Morgan's formative years; and in later life he was to remark that in his schooldays he had been 'more used to the pike than the book'.

Little is known of how Henry Morgan spent the eight years after his arrival with the British invaders in Jamaica. He probably acquired the taste for plantation life which he was not to be able to indulge until relatively old age. He demonstrated his enthusiasm for all things military by joining the Port Royal Regiment as one of its original officers. He must also have participated in some of the privateering voyages which sailed from Port Royal or he would not have been able to raise sufficient following – or sufficient loans – to have achieved his own ship by the time that Commodore Mings was collecting his squadron to attack Santiago in 1662.

Morgan could not have had a better mentor than Mings. The latter assembled and provisioned his expedition with the thoroughness of a true professional. Recruiting parties scoured the alleys and stews of Port Royal for volunteers. Casks of water, flagons of beer, salted pork, fresh fruit and vegetables were all stowed in the holds. Flints were checked on muskets and pistols; pike and sword blades were sharpened. Former prisoners of the Spaniards were questioned about the defences of Santiago. Even when the squadron had sailed, the process of recruiting and collecting intelligence did not end: a vessel commanded by the exiled royalist Sir Thomas Whetstone was encountered and persuaded to join the expedition (Mings was not fussy – he already had privateers sailing under his colours, and now he had an outright pirate) since Whetstone had a number of men on board with first-hand knowledge of the state of the garrison of Santiago. No more was left to chance than need be.

A seventeenth-century map of Port Royal harbour in Jamaica, from which Mings and Morgan sailed on their raid against Santiago

Recognizing the unconventional and irregular nature of his force, Mings set aside the practices of a national navy and adopted those of the brethren of the coast. He did not issue an order of battle but called a council of war. All the thirteen captains – Morgan included – were summoned to his flagship and invited to give their views about the best plan of attack. Santiago was known to be almost impregnable: its Morro Castle commanded the two-hundred-foot-wide channel linking the open sea with the enclosed waters of the harbour. But the assembled buccaneers were reluctant to land down the coast and launch their attack after an overland march: too many of them – like Morgan – remembered the fiasco of Penn landing his force at the wrong place in Hispaniola and Venables bungling his approach march. The assembled captains favoured a bold seaborne assault on the town, disregarding the dangers of the Morro's gun terraces. Mings did not challenge their collective will.

When, however, on 5 October 1662 Mings saw through his eye-glass the ramparts of the Morro at Santiago, he realized that the captains' plan was ill-conceived. Not only was the castle guarding the harbour entrance even stronger than it had been reported to be, but the wind was off-shore and the sea choppy. Sailing in past the shore batteries would be suicidally slow, and standing off shore would risk drifting down past the castle and losing all element of surprise. Mings had been prepared to consult about his plan; he was not prepared to adhere to it in the light of changed circumstances. Realizing that once they were in sight of the enemy only one man could give the orders, Mings decided to put his force ashore two miles to the east of Santiago on the long open beach of Aguadores. (He was subsequently in his report to Lord Windsor to describe the place as 'rocky and narrow', but this must surely have been a reference to the conditions on land and not on the sandy waterfront.)

While Mings had been studying the defences of the Morro through his telescope, the Spanish governor of Santiago had been studying the highly suspect sails which had appeared on the horizon through his. He had no doubt that it was a raiding party from Jamaica, which was only some hundred miles further over the horizon. He called out his militia, set up road blocks between Aguadores and the town, covered the road blocks with cannon, instructed the officer who had been the former Spanish guerrilla leader in Jamaica to take charge of the defences (presumably on the grounds that he knew the mentality of these

The beach of Aguadores where Mings and Morgan landed near
Santiago in Cuba

wild Englishmen), and generally created an atmosphere of alert
and alarm.

Well over a thousand men – regular soldiers, sailors, buccaneers, pirates and Jamaican irregulars – had landed as night
was falling on the beach of Aguadores. They knew they had to
press on rapidly for a dawn attack on Santiago if they were to
stand any chance of overwhelming the garrison, but they had
little idea of the approach route. The only track up from the
beach was wooded and overgrown. Mings was subsequently to
report to Lord Windsor that:

> The path was so narrow that but one man could march at a
> time . . . the way so difficult and the night so dark that our
> guides (had to lead) with brands in their hands to beat the
> path.

As will be found not infrequently in the accounts of the buccaneers' exploits, the actual fighting is passed over in a few sentences in Mings's report. We are told that one Spanish commander and his men 'fairly ran away' and that the Jamaican irregulars 'routed the rest'. Not only was the town of Santiago captured, but six Spanish ships in the harbour were secured before their crews could sail them to safety. Even more surprisingly, the Morro Castle itself capitulated when faced with an unexpected attack from the landward side – one of Mings's subordinates subsequently remarking disdainfully that he could have resisted an assault there indefinitely if accompanied by no other defender than his dog!

The fighting had been brief; the looting took longer. For the next five days the victorious troops plundered the town: silver plate and coin, cannons and kegs of gunpowder, Toledo blades and gilt goblets, bales of hides and barrels of wine . . . all were trundled by the few regular sailors and the many irregular buccaneers down to the Santiago waterfront and loaded on to Mings's original ships and the six additional ones which they had captured and intended to sail home as prizes. This was the moment when so many buccaneering expeditions had gone – and were to go – wrong, when discipline broke, when loathsome brutalities were committed, and when drunkenness took over. Not so when Commodore Mings was in command: destruction and high spirits were to be controlled, but destruction and high spirits there were. Both found their culmination in the blowing up of the famed Morro Castle; seven hundred kegs of gunpowder were devoted to the task and the castle – though rebuilt soon after – was never quite the same again.

Eventually the whole squadron sailed back to Port Royal in triumph. Young captains like Henry Morgan, though hardly rich men, were able to pay off their debts; more importantly, they had seen how such an expedition should be commanded and executed. Some of the lessons had been learnt; others – as we shall see – were never fully to be learnt.

It was clear to me by now that the resurrected Morro Castle and the landing beaches of Aguadores were an essential departure point in any quest to analyse the achievement and retrace the gory path of the man who signed himself Hen: Morgan.

[2]

Life Among the Cays: the Present Day

In the mouth of the harbour the sea was very wild and confused and clear green water was breaking over the rock at the base of the Morro, the tops of the seas blowing white in the sun. It looks wonderful, he said to himself. It not only looks wonderful; it is wonderful. I'm going to have a drink on it. The Floridita was open now . . .*

Havana has a Morro like Santiago, and this was Ernest Hemingway's response to the view across the entrance to Havana harbour – that same view which I enjoyed from the Chancery of the British Embassy. It was also my response one lunch-time as I sat at my desk. I had been there too long. It was time I got out. There was always news and gossip to be picked up at the bar of the Floridita. I would go round there and see what was happening. Maybe there would be Cuban officials at the bar, talking about prospects for the *zafra* – the sugar-cane harvest. Maybe there would be foreign journalists mulling over the latest three-hour speech by Castro. Maybe there would be members of the Cuban national ballet company speculating about whether Alisia Alonso would dance in *Giselle* next week. Certainly there would be the dark shade after the glare of the street, the cool of the air-conditioning after the torrid humidity outside, the long bar where Hemingway had spent so many hours (fifty pages of *Islands in the Stream* alone), and the frozen daiquiris mixed by the successor of Hemingway's Pedrico.

It took a few moments to get used to the darkness, to recognize the framed article from the *New Yorker* describing the Floridita along with the Ritz in Paris and Shepherd's in Cairo as

* *Islands in the Stream* (London, 1970).

one of the world's great bars, to recognize the faded photo-graphs of *Papa* (Hemingway, not Doc), to order a *mulato* (a daiquiri made from dark Cuban rum) and to settle on a high stool with a view down the bar. I had not long to wait for an acquaintance to join me.

'*Que pasa, amigo?* What on earth have you been saying to my Minister?'

Frederico bounded out of the shadows, his booming voice making the glasses on the bar tinkle a thin descant. I recognized him as a senior official of the Cuban fish exporting organization, a large strong man who had been captain of a fishing smack himself in his time, and whose left arm – exposed by his short-sleeved *guayabera* – showed a broad scar which some attributed to an aquatic encounter and others to an incident at the waterside bar at Cojimar.

'The Minister says I'm to arrange for you to go to sea as a crew member of one of our fishing boats . . . no formalities, he says, no protocol . . . says you're interested to see differences be-tween life on a Cuban lobster boat and on a Scottish trawler . . . I told him it was quite impossible of course . . . water too rough . . . living conditions too primitive for an ambassador . . . fishermen's language too undiplomatic . . . why do you want to do it, anyway?'

I remembered my conversation of three weeks before with the Minister of Fisheries. I was, I had said a little pompously, the representative of one fishing nation to another: could I not see something of the Cuban fishing industry at first hand? I had also explained that I was writing a book about the buccaneers and wanted to see something of the cays among which they had sailed. He had looked at me as if assessing my weight/muscle ratio, and he had conferred with his advisers. Would I not prefer to go out on a tourist game-fishing launch? It would be much more 'representational', he suggested. I explained my eccentric request again.

'No one has ever asked to do this before,' the Minister said eventually. 'But if you are really sure you want to go – all right, leave it with me.'

Entrance to Havana harbour today, as seen from the British Embassy

I had not expected to hear any more about it. Now, it seemed, I was to do so.

Frederico settled on a bar stool beside me. He seemed at home there and the barman placed a *mojito* – a long rum drink – unasked in front of him.

'Anyway,' continued Frederico, 'you're on! I've been told to escort you to La Coloma on the south coast of Pinar del Río province and take you out to the cays of San Felipe, and then on down the south coast if you like. You'll see plenty of fishing, get quite a tossing between the cays even if we don't have any more cyclones this season, and hear a few Cuban words you won't find in any dictionary!'

I looked down the long bar and tried to persuade myself that I was a character out of Hemingway to whom these prospects would be all in the day's work. I sipped my daiquiri. Another couple had taken up their post further down the bar: the man thin-lipped and spectacled, the woman tired-looking with her hair in rollers under a head-scarf. Try as I would, I could not see anyone resembling Hemingway's Honest Lil, who

> looked her best when sitting at the far end of the Floridita bar, when you saw only her dark face and the grossness that had come over her body was hidden by the polished wood of the bar.

No, I could not readily transmute myself into a Hemingway environment. The prospect of going to sea as a Cuban fisherman filled me with apprehension, made none the more bearable by the knowledge that my predicament was entirely of my own making.

It was too late for back-tracking. A few days after our chance encounter at the Floridita bar, Frederico and I were trundling through the fields of sugar-cane and the tobacco plantations on our way to La Coloma, a hundred miles south-west of Havana. This little fishing port is the key to the southern cays. Only thirty miles off shore is the string of swampy islands known as the Cays of San Felipe; these reach eastwards towards the great

A Cuban lobster boat of the type on which the author visited the
Cays of San Felipe

island of the southern Cuban shore, the Isle of Pines (renamed
the Isle of Youth by Castro when he set up schools for African
children there); further east again, the broken off-shore islands
merge into the group known as the Jardín de la Reina. This
chain of tiny islands provided a frequent hiding place for
buccaneer ships and a launching pad for their raids on the coast.
From La Coloma they could be explored.

The little port was wholly given over to lobsters. A large
processing plant dominated the quayside. Some four hundred
women worked here handling the catch of the five hundred
fishermen – mostly their own husbands, sons and brothers. The
lobsters were protected for three months a year – March, April
and May – and during that time the fishermen took their
holidays and mended their equipment. For the rest of the year
they were going out to sea, usually for ten days at a time, in the
spartan conditions which I was about to experience.

The ships crowding the river-mouth harbour were lobster

boats of three sorts: *Cayo Largo* or *criollo* wooden boats of some forty or fifty feet in length, or *ferocementos* (concrete boats) of slightly smaller dimensions. Many of the buccaneer boats that made up Mings's, Mansfield's or Morgan's 'fleets' were no larger than these.

The captain of the port walked us round the factory and along the quayside. He was obviously on good terms with Frederico, and I was conscious of being the butt of a number of humorous remarks about diplomats who thought they were sailors. Eventually we stopped by a *criollo* boat, with the scarcely original name of *Caribe* painted in garish colours on its peeling prow. My grip-bag of clothes was tossed aboard. A few cheerful introductions were made as tousled heads appeared from the one hatchway. Frederico and I leapt on to the deck as the engine spluttered to life and I was heading to sea on a Cuban lobster boat. It was only then that I remembered that the sea-sick tablets which I had been recommended and forgotten to swallow – the wind had been getting up ever since we left Havana – took two hours to take effect. As if reading my thought, the master of the *Caribe* said:

'The first two hours will be the worst, after that we get into the shelter of the cays.'

He was right. I preferred to stay on deck rather than face the claustrophobic atmosphere of the one small cabin. But the deck had its hazards. The *Caribe* had only low side rails and as she spiralled through the rough waters – engines at full blast – what little furniture there was on deck rocketed from port to starboard and back; I saw every possibility that not only my chair, but me in it, would disappear over the side – an alarming prospect in the daylight hours and (as I was later to find) a terrifying one at night. I jammed myself into the hatchway entrance by the wheelhouse and hung on.

It seemed much more than two hours before I observed that the darker blue line of the horizon gradually became green; we were approaching the cays of San Felipe. They were not habitable islands, but low banks of mangrove swamp, most of them impenetrable on foot, many of them without fresh water, others dizzy with the buzz of mosquitoes. All of them lay steaming and uninviting in their treacherously shallow surrounding waters. What conceivable attraction had these islands had for Morgan?

One answer is that they were a hiding-place. In the narrow channels between the cays he could anchor his ships concealed from the view of questing Spanish spy-glasses: it was hard to spot a mast, or even the spar of a top-gallant, among the forest of tree-trunks, branches and mangrove. The Cuban cays were still serving the same purpose of concealment when Hemingway's hero of *Islands in the Stream* – Thomas Hudson – was combing the off-shore islands for a Second World War German submarine crew who had stolen a little turtle boat in which to make their escape:

> Hudson studied the cay carefully with the big glasses and saw that the mangroves were too high for him to learn anything about what was inside. There were other trees mixed with the mangroves on the solid part of the cay and they brought the height up even more so that he could not possibly see if there was any mast showing.

It could have been an entry in some Spanish captain's log as he scoured the cays for buccaneer brigantines.

A second reason for Morgan frequenting these cays was that they served as a meeting-place. Joining other ships at sea was a chancy operation for seventeenth-century navigators and timing such a rendezvous was well-nigh impossible. An assembly point on the Cuban coast – even in one of the most deserted bays – was likely to prove hazardous. It was far safer to meet at a landmark off shore which provided cover from view; it was thus that Mings and Morgan met Sir Thomas Whetstone – that renegade nephew of Oliver Cromwell – off the coast before their raid on Santiago, and that Morgan met French privateers on various other occasions.

Lastly, the cays were a happy hunting-ground where small Spanish coastal vessels – fishing craft and pinnaces carrying dispatches from one regional commander to another – could be waylaid. It was from such fortuitous encounters that Morgan derived intelligence of the Spanish defences of Santiago and other targets on mainland Cuba. No wonder then that the cays of San Felipe and those further eastward were a favourite haunt not only for Morgan but for his predecessors and successors.

Showing once again an almost uncanny capacity to echo my

Life at sea among the Cuban cays

own thoughts, the Master of our fishing vessel said: 'Good place for hiding, these cays.' He then went on to tell me tales – which I am sure he believed – of clandestine activities based on the cays: illicit landings, drug smuggling, infiltration by saboteurs and other piratical activities which might well have stimulated the imagination of the most lively buccaneer. One gathered the cays were as rife with nefarious activity now as at any time over the intervening centuries.

Certainly the cays were alive with maritime movement. Small craft resembling our own nosed out from the cover of the mangroves; on closer inspection all of them turned out to be engaged in nothing more villainous than lobster fishing. The process involved many boats and much labour. In the shallow waters near the cays, corrals were erected on the bed of the sea – long funnels of fencing leading into cages. At certain seasons and in certain weathers the lobster would be 'on the march'. As they moved along the sea bottom they would come up against a netting fence which they could not penetrate, and would follow it until they were led into the cage, which might be ten yards in diameter and marked with tall stakes to make it visible above the surface. The lobster boats would ply between these corrals, dropping off – in a rowing-boat with an outboard motor – two men at a time, who would jump into the corrals and toss the live lobsters out into the rowing-boat, returning to their larger craft to tranship them. Then the fishing boats – ones like my own – would take their cargo to lobster gathering stations. These were built on stilts in the shallows and seemed securely enough constructed. But in reality they too were hazardous in a strong wind and lethal in a hurricane. In fact, when hurricane-force winds were forecast, the port captain at La Coloma would send a boat to evacuate all the lobster stations. Twice within the few months before my visit the station on which we landed had been totally destroyed: the strong planks of the jetty and the board-ing of the cabin – in which seven men would normally sleep – had been smashed to matchwood in the first minutes of the storms.

Here at the gathering stations, the lobsters were weighed and credited to the boat crews who brought them in. They were separated into large, medium and small sizes, and finally they were tossed into underwater cages attached to the sides of the wooden platforms that made up the station. Woe betide the lobster that was inadvertently lodged with larger cell-mates, as it would be eaten by its fellows. Eventually, a slightly larger boat would collect the harvest from the gathering station and take it back – still alive – to the factory at La Coloma which I had seen before embarkation.

The work at all stages was arduous and not infrequently dangerous. Although Cuban lobsters have no claws, it is not easy or pleasant work plucking them from the seething nets of the corrals. Men who slip in the chest-high water can be attacked by scores of lobsters thrusting their antennae – the substitute for claws – into their eyes and other sensitive parts. And life on the boats is hard for the ten days and nights that they stay at sea: in the one cabin, with its narrow bunks and communal existence, little seemed to have changed from the life that Morgan's seamen would have recognized.

At irregular intervals, bearing no particular relationship to the time of day, the oldest of the seamen, Angel, brought us food, which was almost invariably fresh lobster – delicious and needing no sauces – or whatever other fish we had caught. Angel had clearly been relegated to cooking from harder physical work, but his advice was promptly sought whenever difficulties arose: when we went aground, as happened from time to time in the shallow channels, it was he who was called to the wheelhouse to suck his few remaining teeth and suggest what to do next. When thus installed in the wheelhouse, Angel's wrinkled face did not express emotion like other faces: not for him were frowns and puckered brows when crises threatened. But as he sucked his teeth the matchstick which rested permanently in the corner of his mouth – a sort of cigarette substitute – began to move to and fro across his mouth: the speed at which this tiny fragment of timber travelled was the only indicator of tension. For tensions there were. On those occasions when the ship went aground, the conversation closely resembled the dialogue in

Islands in the Stream when Hudson is grounded in a narrow channel in another group of Cuban cays:

> 'Both wheels are sound. She's just in mud up to her ass.'
> 'I know, I put her there.'
> 'She'll come off as easy as she went in.'
> 'Sure she will.'

And so on; and so on. The language of the sea changes little in these parts.

Nor do the stories. As we fished in the fading evening light – the best time for casting a line over the side – I would be regaled with tales of the deep and, even more, of the shallows. I was told how spraying water over the side from a hose with a fine rose nozzle made a noise like *bonitos* eating, and so brought fish to the surface ready to snap at even a bare hook in these unsuspecting waters. One evening I caught a small barracuda and we examined its ferociously protruding jaws.

'The meanest of fish,' said Angel, kicking off his worn canvas shoes to reveal two missing toes.

'That happened off this very cay,' he said. 'Two years ago, when I was still working the lobster nets, I saw the fish were restive one evening and guessed that there were barracuda about. So I climbed back into the boat, and just as I was heaving myself over the side something caught at my boot . . . thought it was a net or some weed . . . so I just pulled . . . wasn't till I was into the boat that I saw the whole toe-cap of the boot was missing . . . and a couple of toes of mine inside it. Lucky it wasn't my leg. Just like barracuda to attack when your back's turned. Mean fish they are.'

He gave my catch a kick with his diminished foot.

On one occasion I experienced an unusually sharp tug on my fishing line. I hoped it would prove to be a red snapper – the most desirable of the likely catch. But after a few moments my quarry broke the surface and revealed itself as an *agujon* – literally translated, 'a hat-pin' – thin, silvery and most of its three-foot length appearing to be teeth. With difficulty I landed

Angel, the Cuban fisherman who befriended the author

the fish on the deck and it snapped at our ankles like an angry corgi. I hopped out of its way, calling to my shipmates to help me club the *agujon* over the head.

When all was calm again, Angel said: 'How would you have liked it if that had been a shark you had landed?'

'I wouldn't have been either strong enough or silly enough to land a shark on deck,' I replied.

'You don't always have the choice. We were pulling in a net

one day in a heavy, rolling sea off the Jardín de la Reina cays
when the whole starboard deck went under water . . . when the
ship righted itself again there was a hammerhead shark trapped
on deck . . . never seen fishermen move faster. . . .' The
matchstick fairly raced across Angel's gnarled mouth at the
mere recollection of the drama.

Much to my embarrassment, it was I who produced the
liveliest drama of this voyage. We had anchored off the southern shore of one of the smaller cays; the day was hot and airless
even by Cuban standards; everyone was fishing for red snapper
until it was time to make the late afternoon round of the lobster
corrals. I decided I would swim out and snorkel off a clearly
visible coral reef a couple of hundred yards away, where Angel
said there was a wreck below the surface.

In these waters, so free until now from the attentions of
marine archaeologists, it was always possible that the wreck was
a seventeenth-century one. Indeed, only a few days before
leaving Havana a European treasure-hunting firm had
approached me about obtaining permission for them to dive in
these waters. How better to spend a sweltering afternoon than
in carrying out my own reconnaissance?

With mask and flippers adjusted, I prepared to set out. When
Angel saw me about to go over the side, he told me to wait a
moment; he went below and returned with a long wooden-
shafted spear or harpoon.

'Always as well to be prepared,' he said. 'Remember what I
told you about mean fish.'

The spear had a barbed metal head and a leather thong, near
the blunt end, which Angel bound round my wrist so that I
would not lose it. Thus equipped I set off for my wreck.

I cannot claim that I made any substantial discovery: no
galleon of the Spanish plate fleet was to be located by me that
steaming afternoon. But I was on to something, before disaster
overtook me. I had reached the coral reef without difficulty and,
following a practice learnt on the reefs near Havana, I waited
until I spotted a shoal of translucent blue angel-fish; then I
followed them, confident that they would wend their way

through the deepest channels in the reef to the hidden lagoons within. Soon I was swimming in clear water over a sandy bottom twenty feet below me, with banks of bright yellow 'brain' coral encircling the lagoon.

It was then that I saw what looked like a corner of a wooden chest jutting out of the sand. It might have been no more than a fish box for all I could see, but it seemed to warrant further investigation, so I made a short and unsuccessful dive to reach it – or at least come within spear range of it.

On the way up to the surface past a wall of coral, riddled like a honeycomb with crevices, I spied a sinister green face peering out at me. It was so venomous in appearance that my reflex action was to take a jab at it with my spear. Something grabbed the wooden shaft just below the barb. As I rose to the surface the spear was held firm below me, and I in turn was attached by the wrist to the spear.

Happily my head was already above the surface when the leather thong linking me with the spear went taut. I was anchored to whatever had grabbed the spear shaft.

With one arm held stretched below me by the leather thong, I gyrated on the surface, peering down through my goggle mask to see what was detaining me. What I saw was not reassuring. Stretching nearly three feet out of the crevice was the green, ridged, tube-like body of something looking like a snake. Its head, green and strangely shaggy, was fastened by vicious-looking teeth to the woodwork of my weapon. Its tail disappeared into the depths of the crevice where I had first seen its eyes. I suspected – rightly – that the tip of its tail was entwined round some piece of coral giving it a firm, well-nigh unbreakable grip.

Even at this moment I realized how much worse – how fatal, in fact – it would have been if it had been my arm or leg and not my long-handled spear that the creature had bitten. The agony and danger of the bite apart, my arm or leg would have been held six feet below the surface and I would undoubtedly have drowned before I could release myself.

As it was, I fumbled at the leather thong. The sea water had made it swell. I could only use my left hand to try to undo it. I was getting nowhere. I splashed around in circles, my right arm still stretched beneath me, like a porpoise on a chain. I was just beginning to wonder what would happen next when I spotted Angel at the oars of the *Caribe*'s dinghy, striking out with rapid strokes in my direction. When he came alongside he did not stop to hear my somewhat incoherent explanation of my predicament. He reached down into the water with a knife in his hand and cut the leather thong. Watching his prized spear sink, he could see through the clear blue water the cause of my trouble.

'You're a lucky man,' he said. 'Do you know what it was that grabbed you? It was a moray eel – in fact a green moray, the worst sort of all. They never let go. Don't bother about the harpoon. Jump in the boat.'

On my way back to the *Caribe* I decided that my mysterious wooden box in the lagoon could stay mysterious for a little longer: a green moray was as good a sentinel as Cerberus as far as I was concerned!

Frederico and I were transhipped at a lobster station on to a larger vessel that would take us past the Isle of Pines and eastwards down the string of cays and islands towards Santiago de Cuba: Morgan's destination had to be mine too. We came upon the entrance to the harbour in the evening light, with a fresh off-shore breeze against us. These were the very conditions that had deterred Commodore Mings from taking his squadron straight in to attack the town as his captains had planned to do. We however were impervious to his constraints: making full use of our powerful engines, and with nothing to fear from the gun terraces of the Morro Castle looming above us in the narrow harbour entrance, we slipped under the towering walls, well appreciating as we did so the temerity of what Mings's commanders had originally intended to do.

One of the joys of travel is immersing oneself in a different society, with different everyday values from one's own. This – thanks to the Cuban Minister of Fisheries – I had been able to do during these past days and nights. I pondered on it as we prepared to land. How had these rough Cuban seamen's values differed from those of the urbane world of diplomacy from which I had temporarily defected? It was tempting to say that they held life and limb more cheaply than does sophisticated society: to see in them some common outlook with the swash-buckling ruffians who had faced many of the same dangers in the same waters three centuries earlier. Tempting, but mis-leading. Life and limb had not been held cheap by those among whom I had been living: a lost shipmate, a lost leg, even a couple of lost toes . . . these were setbacks not easily absorbed; but they were a price that might at any moment have to be paid for things held dearer still – a livelihood for their families, a harvest from the sea for their country, the respect of their comrades. I landed at Santiago less well-shaven than I had set out, and less certain about some of the judgements I had so firmly expounded in Havana. Life among the cays had not quite fitted into the pattern I had prescribed for it.

The next day I said farewell to Frederico and was joined by Caroline – my wife – who had flown down from Havana. We determined to reapproach Santiago by the route taken by Mings and Morgan, that is, from the bay of Aguadores a few miles to the east of the town. We made various false starts.

The eastern provinces of Cuba, of which Santiago is still the principal city, were suffering from an outbreak of African swine fever. Everywhere pigs were dying. The infection was spread-ing alarmingly. Precautions to contain the disease had been decreed by the authorities. Road blocks were set up and car tyres were sprayed while passengers were made to disembark and walk through troughs of chemicals to disinfect their shoes. We took an easterly road out of Santiago and soon were undergoing the prescribed process.

'Where are your other shoes?' asked the policeman.

'In my suitcase,' said Caroline, 'but I've just arrived by air from Havana and there's no swine fever there.'

'May I see them, please?'

The boot was opened; a suitcase was opened; some delicate evening shoes ('Santiago isn't very Ritzy', I had said, but evening shoes had been packed none the less) and bedroom slippers emerged.

'Please to walk through the trough in them,' said our policeman in a deadpan voice.

Reluctantly Caroline obliged, putting on first her ordinary shoes, then her evening shoes, then her bedroom slippers at one end of the trough and taking them off at the other.

'Why do you want to go down this road anyway?' asked the policeman when all the perambulating had finished.

'We're going to Aguadores,' I explained.

'But this isn't the road to Aguadores; you should have turned right a kilometre back.'

'Thank you,' I said, 'we'll go back.'

'Please, then, the lady to walk through the trough again.'

'But I've only just gone through it,' Caroline remonstrated.

'Everyone walking through trough in both directions,' said the policeman stolidly.

'Surely that's if you've walked somewhere else in between?'

'Everyone walking through trough in both directions.'

'But these bedroom slippers will be ruined by all this unnecessary paddling: you've *seen* I've not walked anywhere in them since I last went through!'

'Everyone walking through . . .'

'Look,' I said, intervening as one reasonable man to another. 'These are my wife's *bedroom* slippers; she's not likely to have picked up this fever of yours going to bed.'

'Fever . . . going to bed . . . the lady is not well?'

'No, listen,' I said. 'It's her *slippers* that could pick up the fever, not her.'

'Yes, yes . . . slippers pick up fever . . . please to go through . . . everyone walking through trough . . .'

Caroline splashed back again.

We retraced our route for a kilometre and found that the policeman had been accurate enough about the dirt road leading down to the bay of Aguadores. Soon we abandoned the car and took to the rocky, bramble-covered path that led steeply down to the long, wide beach. This was the path that Mings, Morgan and their men had had to negotiate in the dark. We were not surprised to note from Mings's own account to Lord Windsor that his men had had to go single file and had been obliged to stop and kindle a fire so that those in front could carry flaming brands to light the way for those behind. As we stumbled and slid in broad daylight, we did not envy them their night-time ascent.

The beach itself, when we reached it, was deserted apart from a few long-disused fishing boats. Rocks and coral off shore made the approaches uninviting. Even the small rowing-boats which would have been used as landing-craft must have had difficulty in reaching the beach intact, and no wonder many of the men wading ashore had kept their powder and flint-locks dry only with the greatest difficulty.

But there appeared to have been even worse hazards. As we looked back from the beach at the overgrown path down which we had come, we were surprised to see, peeping through the foliage on the rocky crags flanking the path, stone turrets and fragments of battlements denoting fortifications. We clambered up to them, molested as we climbed by the attentions of a giant hawk whose nest we may well have been appearing to menace. Wings flapped close to our faces as we grasped at roots and rocks; a hooked beak swept unpleasantly close to our eyes as we fumbled for footholds.

When we reached the line of masonry, there was no doubt about its antiquity. These were seventeenth-century defences. How curious that the Spanish had not managed to stem the advance of the buccaneers from this vantage point. How even more curious that it had not been mentioned in Mings's account of his landing. The explanation seemed likely to be that the turrets and battlements along which we were scrambling had been built *after* Mings's raid – that they had in fact been an example of shutting the stable door after the horse had bolted. (We were to find numerous similar examples round the Caribbean of such 'too late' constructions – notably the walls of Campeche – in the wake of Captain Morgan.)

We descended from the defences by a different route and set

out to retrace overland the line of Mings's advance on the Morro at Santiago. Like him, we followed the coastline as closely as we could. The landward approach to the Morro – now as then – is open countryside unencumbered by buildings; the fortress stands on its headland overlooking the narrow entrance channel to the harbour with nothing around it but a green swath. Once the moat must have been full; now that it is empty it looks all the deeper. The bridge across had a locked gate and there was no gate-keeper, nor any place from which we could enquire about finding the key.

It seemed a pity to have got so far and to be frustrated from entering the formidable Morro. While Caroline attempted to find some good angles for photography, I reconnoitred the ground. A stone parapet was easily vaulted; the locked gate proved no great obstacle to climb. Like Henry Morgan, I had penetrated the forbidden Morro.

It was strangely spooky. Stone corridors gave on to more stone corridors; corners revealed sharp flights of steps leading downwards to darkness; magnificent views of the bay alternated with scaringly sheer drops to the sea. I strayed into a room arranged as a museum with glass cases displaying 'trophies of pirates ancient and modern': cutlasses and spyglasses dating from the seventeenth century were among the former, and supposedly CIA automatics and binoculars dating from the twentieth century among the latter. I felt guilty at prying in so unauthorized a way on these ill-assorted relics, some of the earlier of them captured from my own compatriots.

It was then that I heard the footsteps descending the stone staircase behind me. The loneliness of the place and my bad conscience at my intrusion induced something akin to panic. I ran down a further flight of stone steps disappearing at an angle into yet more profound gloom. I dreaded the explanations and embarrassments of discovery. In my haste I passed a heavy oak doorway and arrived in a cell illuminated only by a three-inch slit in the thick masonry of the wall.

One has often read memoirs of people incarcerated in

dungeons vile: my own first such impressions were based on the adventures of Toad in *The Wind in the Willows*. When I heard the heavy iron-studded oak door which I had passed only moments before clang shut behind me, and a creaking lock turn, I knew how Toad had felt, how the inmates of the Bastille or the Tower had felt. I was alone, entombed in the dark bowels of a *château fort*.

I tried to pull myself together and rationalize the situation. Who had locked me in, and why? Clearly the steps I had heard had been those of a curator or guardian. He could not know I was there. He must have been engaged in a routine lock-up. Caroline was outside. If I did not reappear, eventually she would institute a search. I had only to bide my time in patience: a fitting penalty for an impatient entry into premises which – by the most charitable interpretation – had not been conspicuously open to the public.

Time hangs heavily in dark, stone cells. I fell to wondering if compatriots of mine had languished here in the years before Mings and Morgan had come to their rescue. It was all too likely. Sometimes Morgan and his men had released west-country seamen who had spent decades in Spanish dungeons: when he captured the Royal Treasury at Portobello, a few years after Santiago, Morgan found eleven Englishmen, chained to the walls of a dungeon not much more than ten foot square, who had been there for more than two years; emaciated and half blind, their wrists and ankles chafed raw by their fetters, they had been scarcely recognizable as former mariners. Indeed, on that occasion Morgan had hoped that he might find and release Prince Maurice, a nephew of Charles I of England, who had disappeared – assumed to have been captured and incarcerated – some five years previously.

Daylight was fading and the thin pencil of illumination from the slit in my cell wall was all but extinguished. A bell chimed somewhere far above me, and I remembered how the Spanish practice of sounding an alarm bell when their forts were under assault had put fresh cheer into the hearts of their captives. It encouraged me to think that even now Caroline might be

The Morro at Santiago, Cuba

persuading some grumpy custodian to retrace his rounds and unlock his inadvertent prisoner's door.

More time passed. It had long ago become too dark to read the face of my watch. I had no matches. Then – quite suddenly – I heard the relief forces coming.

'Yes, officer, I think I may have dropped it going down these dark steps . . . how silly of me . . . let's have a look with my torch . . . perhaps this door was open before . . . may I borrow your key for a moment, officer?' Caroline's Spanish was unmistakable.

The lock ground open as creakily as it had closed.

'Are you there? Thank God!' This time Caroline was whispering in English. 'Slip out quickly up the stairs to the right while I go on pretending to look for my hotel key. If they catch you, you're for it. Apparently it's still military premises.'

I needed no further encouragement. The moon was up and I

could just make out the route by which I had entered. Never had captive left his cell with more alacrity. Behind me I could hear Caroline still talking to the custodian. It seemed her key was found; thanks and tips were being offered, the former accepted and the latter declined (in accordance with almost invariable Cuban practice).

When we were safely back, reunited and alone together on the green swath in front of the Morro, and I had been reprimanded for my adventure, I told Caroline about the coincidence of hearing the bell chiming just before she came to my rescue.

She looked at me quizzically: 'There's only one thing odd about that: the bell-tower was blown down in a hurricane and the custodian told me they took the bell into Santiago three years ago.'

Perhaps those seventeenth-century English intruders had left something behind them less concrete than arms and spyglasses, chains and fetters? Perhaps I had come closer than I knew to the spirit of those buccaneers whose exploits I so feebly emulated.

3

Raids on Mexico: 1660s and 1980s

Henry Morgan was involved in two separate raiding expeditions into Mexico – New Spain as it was then called – in 1663 and 1664.

The first was, once more, under command of Commodore Christopher Mings, who had led the Santiago de Cuba raid. Mings maintained to the Governor and Council of Jamaica that he had two justifications for a further raid on a Spanish settlement. The principal one was – as in the case of Santiago – that King Charles II's instructions remained that his subjects should 'procure a trade by force' with the Spanish possessions. The Santiago experience did not appear to have effected any change of heart in the Spanish authorities: no mercantile approaches were made by them, and all English approaches remained rebuffed. Mings managed to persuade the Governor that if commercial openings were to be made, they would have to be – as it were – blasted open: a curious variant of the philosophy that trade follows the flag.

The second justification was perhaps even more tortuous. Mings maintained that a raid on the coast of New Spain – particularly on the southern coast of what is now called the Gulf of Mexico – would give succour and support to the only English community on the Spanish Main. This was a series of small timber-felling settlements along the Gulf shore between the Yucatán peninsula and the already well-established Spanish city of Veracruz. The logwood cutters – as they were called – were a tough lot, beholden to no one and doling out a rough and ready justice among themselves. Their presence was, of course, unacceptable to the Spaniards; they managed to exist only because of the inaccessibility of the region in which they lived and worked. The stretch of coast in question was unapproach-able by land on account of the vast tract of salt flats, mangrove swamps and forests which lay behind it. It was also difficult to approach from the sea as shallows, cays and reefs made the off-shore waters a navigator's nightmare. But the hard, straight timber had a high value, and intrepid English sea captains (as well as occasional Frenchmen and Dutchmen) put in on this coast and bartered provisions, clothes, firearms and rum for the logwood. Mings maintained that a feat of arms by him and his associates on this stretch of coast would demonstrate, both to the Spaniards and to the logwood cutters, that there was a formidable English presence in the region and that it was well to leave his compatriots in peace to ply their axes and their barter unmolested by the land or sea power of Spain.

Having established these patriotic objectives, Mings looked around for a rich prize worth the plundering. He settled on San Francisco de Campeche, almost in the middle of the logwood cutters' stretch of the Gulf and the most prosperous town on that coast. Campeche had been built by the Spaniards on a Mayan site of that name. Because it had never been attacked before, Mings imagined that its defences would be weak: a somewhat rash assumption. In fact, Campeche not only had a garrison of regular Spanish troops, but it was guarded by two formidable citadels each situated on a commanding hill: the Castillo San Miguel two miles to the south, and the Castillo San José two miles to the north. There were also three batteries of cannon between the citadels and in front of the town, but the state of the town's perimeter walls is uncertain, and they may have been far from sound. However, Mings was less concerned with such practical details than with his estimate of the prizes likely to be found there. He calculated that, as the major port of call between Veracruz and Havana, Campeche was likely to harbour at any given moment a number of Spanish merchant-men with valuable cargoes; he could also be confident that the townsfolk of such a well-founded community would have accumulated silver and coin.

Persuading the brethren of the coast of the potentially lucrative nature of the venture proved a good deal easier than persuading the Governor and Council of the national interest that the expedition would achieve. Mings's reputation was high. Those who had served under him on the Santiago raid had returned not only enriched but impressed by their commander's naval and military skills. Among the captains of some dozen privateer vessels to offer their services were the young Henry Morgan and his friend (and subsequent lieutenant) John Morris. French ships arrived from Tortuga, and some Dutch privateers were also issued with letters of marque for the expedition. In all it was some score of ships, carrying a force of more than a thousand men, which sailed under Mings's flag from Port Royal on 12 January 1663.

Mings, on his flagship the *Centurion*, led his multinational fleet past the western tip of Cuba, through the Yucatán channel, round the western side of the Yucatán peninsula and along the eastern shore of the Gulf of Mexico until he reached the latitude of Campeche. Estimating the distance down that stretch of coastline cannot have been easy. The whole of Yucatán is a sedimented limestone plateau into which the rainwater sinks to subterranean reservoirs; no rivers run into the sea, and thus there are no tell-tale streaks of muddy water issuing out from the land as indications of how far the navigator has reached down the coast. What charts there were of the Main were mostly of Spanish compilation and unlikely to have been available to the brethren of the coast. Mings, Morgan and their fellow adventurers had sailed some thousand miles before they turned inshore, braving the shoals of the Bay of Campeche, to sight their objective exactly where they had calculated it to be.

The buccaneers were never lacking in effrontery. Mings's first action was neither reconnaissance nor attack: it was to send a boat ashore with a peremptory demand for the surrender of the Spanish town. The governor – secure behind his garrison, his citadels and his batteries – did not deign to reply. But he was not so inviolable as he imagined. The roundshot from the citadels could not reach ships anchored off the port; the town walls were incomplete and in bad repair; the morale of the garrison was shaken by the unexpected appearance of a hostile fleet, and – as it turned out – the batteries of cannon defending the town were too close to the seafront and vulnerable to sudden assault.

Mings waited as long as he dared for the Spaniards to reply, but could not afford to give them time to reorganize themselves. Once he had decided on attack, rapidity was a vital ingredient of success. He therefore embarked his men in the ships' boats and, endeavouring to keep their flint-lock muskets, pistols and powder dry, they soon made their landing. Henry Morgan and the other captains went ashore in the first wave with their men, many of whom were armed only with swords, pikes or daggers. The batteries were soon overpowered, and the defenders fell back into the narrow streets of the town itself. Little was reported by Mings about the nature of the hand-to-hand fighting that followed, except that it went on all day.

By nightfall all resistance was broken and the plundering had begun. Casualties on both sides had been light. Mings's calculations about the likelihood of Spanish merchantmen being in harbour proved justified; there were fourteen of them. With the shore batteries in his hands, he prevented them leaving the port and sent prize crews on board. His calculation about the riches of the citizens also appears to have been correct; the attack had been so sudden that there had been insufficient time to secrete the plate, lace and even jewels. No torturing of well-heeled burghers or their servants seems to have been necessary, only a thorough search at pike-point.

The much-augmented fleet that sailed back to Port Royal was manned by a well-rewarded and well-contented body of buccaneers. If under Mings's command at Santiago and Campeche so much could be achieved for such relatively little loss, the younger commanders such as Morgan argued, why should they not launch out on their own? Much had been learnt about how to raise a crew, how to navigate in dangerous and hostile waters, how to achieve surprise, how to press home an attack. Participation at Campeche had been an illuminating experience for young Captain Henry Morgan.

Clearly Campeche was a place I had to visit if we were to follow Morgan's important and formative expeditions. The small town is – now as then – capital of its own province of Mexico; but unlike Merida, the capital of the neighbouring province of Yucatán, it has no international airport and none of the tourist activity generated by the famous Mayan archaeological sites of Yucatán. The old part of the town of Campeche remains a quiet backwater, unremarkable by cosmopolitan standards and inaccessible without a difficult journey.

As the first stage in the journey, Caroline and I flew from Havana to Merida. We had to spend a day there arranging our onward journey overland; and Merida was a slight disappointment. We had expected too much. We had, to start with, expected it to resemble that Merida in the Estremadura region of Spain after which the conquistadors had named it, but it was hotter and noisier, more spread out and more brash. It was as if the old Spanish town we loved had got overblown in the tropics.

Water wagon in Merida, Mexico

We found the bus depot on the outskirts of the town, and waited at the booking counter while a sulky-faced girl completed her make-up, adding rouge to her dark cheeks and achieving a curiously oriental look, before she attended to the queue of prospective travellers. There were, it appeared, two routes to Campeche. We could either go by the western road, or by a slightly longer eastern road which passed by the celebrated Mayan ruins of Uxmal. We opted for the latter. To forgo a chance of seeing Uxmal would have been like passing Luxor in a night steamer up the Nile.

When we got to the bus the next morning, we discovered that we had been given the cramped back seats over the wheels. Doubtless Mexicans would have recognised the tell-tale seat numbers on the ticket, but as foreigners we had been fair game on which to unload them. Wistfully we thought of our bus journeys across Eastern Turkey* on which as foreigners we had invariably been given the coveted front seats behind the driver. We struggled our way down the narrow centre passage of the bus, reminded as we did so of a comment by Graham Greene on Mexican manners: 'People never seem to help each other in small ways, removing a parcel from a seat, making room with their legs. They just sit about.'**

But we were wrong to be resentful. As we travelled through the flat, wooded Yucatán scenery, our companions started extending small courtesies: a boiled sweet from one, a helpful adjustment of the window from another. This was the true and friendly face of Mexico. And then, after a little over an hour, we turned off the road and halted at Uxmal.

The moment you draw up at Uxmal you see the main sight: the elliptical Pyramid of the Magician, which towers over the half-mile-square complex of temples, palaces and courtyards. The name of this pyramid had some foundation in Mayan folklore, but most of the names by which the individual ruins are known were devised by their Spanish discoverers and relate to buildings of which they reminded the Spaniards, rather than

* See the author's *The Trail of Tamerlane* (London, 1980)
** *The Lawless Roads* (London, 1939)

to what they really were. Thus the huge stone quadrangle, with its colonnades and arches, is dubbed the Nunnery, though Mayan nuns are an improbable concept and this particular building was unlikely to have been set aside for sacrificial virgins (whose occupation might have given some tenuous validity to the name).

Although only a hundred feet high, the Pyramid of the Magician appears far taller on account of the steepness of its sides. The steps to the summit are at an angle well in excess of forty-five degrees. We sat down with a cool drink and watched others going up and down. At some moments everyone would appear relaxed, climbing up with cheerful determination and walking down confidently facing outwards. At other moments everyone would appear nervous, struggling up apprehensively and descending facing inwards and anxiously gripping the chain provided as a banister. Vertigo, we decided, is a contagious disease.

And everywhere we looked: sun on stone, sun on stone. There is a harshness about the quality of Mexican sunshine which is mirrored in the roughness of the stone that reflects it. One is dazzled and cannot focus. Mayans, Toltecs, Aztecs . . . these peoples with their unblinking, expressionless faces, with their feathered serpent gods, with their carved eagles devouring human hearts . . . they stared out from their ruins at us across an abyss of non-comprehension. It was time we moved on to Campeche, to the traces of a seventeenth-century European culture to which we could respond, for whose cruelties we could at least blush.

Another hour and a half and we were there. The centre of Campeche nestles within its seventeenth-century walls which, though not complete, still boast well-preserved corner bastions. Our first question was: how had Mings, Morgan and their men managed to force an entry at all? We were still asking it as we inspected the small museum built into the walls themselves on the seaward side. Here were swords and pistols, muskets and pikes – possibly the very ones which had been used to defend the town against Mings. Here too were portraits of Morgan and the other buccaneers who had raided Campeche. There were also plans of the town and models of the fortresses. It was the plans that answered our question. The present walls had not been constructed until *after* Mings's raid of 1663; indeed, like the fortifications on the beach at Aguadores, they had been built as a direct consequence of it to try to ensure against any repetition.

None the less, we walked around the walls and photographed the main gateway and the corner bastions. Campeche – like Merida – had been constructed on a grid system: even-numbered streets directly intersected odd-numbered ones. Many of the houses, like the walls, were built of solid stone. Now we found the answer to our second question: having entered the town so easily, why had it take a thousand buccaneers a whole day to subdue the resistance? The reason was that each house had been a miniature fortress and had been manned by the retreating Spanish soldiers; and each straight street had provided a clear line of fire. Solid buildings and direct fields of fire favour the defenders. Campeche was a tough nut to crack and must have demanded discipline as well as resolution from Mings's men.

We have an unexpected witness to the sentiments Mings inspired in – of all people – Samuel Pepys, who was no lover of buccaneers. Pepys reported in his diary on 8 June 1666 that a certain Sir Christopher Mings had been 'shot through the face, and into the shoulder, where the bullet lodged', in a naval battle with the Dutch. Mings died of these wounds, and Pepys not only attended his funeral but gave some account of this entirely self-made man, whose 'father being always, and at this day, a shoemaker, and his mother a hoyman's daughter, of which he used frequently to boast', later 'was come into great renowne in the West Indies'. At the funeral Pepys was approached by a dozen 'able, lusty, proper men' who offered their services to man a fireship and thus revenge their dead commander; he was so moved by this display of affection that he 'could hardly abstain from weeping' and commented that Mings was 'a very stout man, a man of great parts, and most excellent tongue

The old walls of Campeche, Mexico

among ordinary men'. Mings had needed all those qualities of leadership and common touch in the course of that fierce day's fighting at Campeche just three years earlier.

It was late lunchtime when we completed our tour, and Caroline – ever alert to a good restaurant – had already spotted one on the seaward side of the town to which we could repair. Mexican food is prepared in the expectation that it will be doused in hot tabasco sauce; the bottles stand on the table in readiness, like tomato ketchup in a British fish-and-chip shop. This does not encourage delicacy of flavouring, but neither does it mean that the food is necessarily as awful as Graham Greene found it: 'like the food you eat in a dream, tasteless in a positive way, so that the very absence of taste is repellent . . . if it isn't hot with sauces, it isn't anything at all'.

In fact, we were discovering that Mr Greene was a prejudiced witness on many aspects of Mexican life: he had not liked the country, and for good reason. The task that had brought him here in 1938 was to find out how the ordinary people had reacted to the brutal anti-clerical purges of President Calles. His travels had mostly been in the tropical states of Chiapas and Tabasco (where we were to go ourselves on the next leg of our journey in pursuit of Morgan) and he had found churches destroyed or closed, and priests driven out or shot. It had been a difficult, bitter and depressing experience, though one from which he was to emerge enriched and on which he was to base first his travel book *The Lawless Roads* and then his celebrated novel *The Power and the Glory*. So there is a sour flavour to his comments; while we, for our part, loved the country.

We ordered our lunch: *ceviche* (raw fish marinated in lemon juice), followed by a sort of *shashlik* with little tomatoes, and topped off with mango ice-cream. Mr Greene would not have approved; he had characteristically been told, 'you're all right if you don't eat fish. Or meat. Or vegetables.' We had hardly completed our order when we were hailed across the restaurant.

'You two are Brits, aren't you?'

A large florid man strode across the room and plonked himself at our table. Caroline confessed we were British.

'First thing you need's a glass of the local poison. *Tres tequilas, pronto!*' he called to the overworked waiter, and duly three glasses arrived (to be duly put on my bill).

'Well, well. Small world. Or had you been told you'd find me here around the witching hour? Barraclough's the name. Jim Barraclough.'

We shook hands awkwardly, as Englishmen do when surprised in unexpected places.

'Always on the lookout for anyone from the old country who may need a spot of help,' said Mr Barraclough. 'Sort of British Consul, you might say.'

'You're the Honorary Consul, perhaps?' I enquired innocently.

'Well, now. We have to choose our words carefully, don't we? That's what I'm known as: yes. Jim Barraclough, the chap who looks after Brits and British interests in these parts. But those Embassy chappies in Mexico City wrote me a stuffy letter a year or two ago: something about not sailing under borrowed colours. It's not me who borrows them, old boy. Can't help it if *they* all call me Mr Great Britain round here, can I?'

He jerked his head towards the room full of Mexicans with an implication that they were busy nailing Union Jacks on him.

'What can I do for you? Want an intro to a decent pub to stay at? Or if you need a taxi, I know a chap who's less of a robber than most of them.'

We explained that we were only in Campeche for one night. We had a hotel. We had already managed to find and photograph the old walls. We were sure we would have no problem getting a taxi at the Presidente Hotel to take us the two miles out to the Castillo San Miguel in the cool of the evening. We should

The coat of arms of the city of
Campeche in the Spanish imperial
period

be siesta-ing meanwhile. It was kind of him to offer his assistance, but really . . . we tried to sound like independent,
self-sufficient travellers.

'So when you've had your lunch you're signing off for an hour
or two. Right. Quite right. In this bloody climate a spot of
Egyptian PT – as we used to call it in the Regiment – is the only
way to get through the p.m. "Studying for the Staff College" –
that's what I used to say as I sloped off to my pit after tiffin in the
Mess.'

I felt that some bonhomie was called for from our side, as a
prelude to disengaging.

'I believe that in the RAF,' I said, 'they describe it as
"climbing to two and a half feet and then levelling out".'

'I like it!' he bellowed. 'I like it a lot! Can't let you slip off
before you've told me a few more good ones like that. Tell you
what: I'll come round to your hotel at five and bring Pedro and
his jalopy along. He'll save you a fortune on the run out to San
Miguel and I'll be able to show you some of the bits they don't
normally let foreigners see.'

With that, inadvertently downing the last of Caroline's
drink, he was off with a cheery wave.

After our siesta, we tried to find a back exit from the hotel
without success, and when we eventually emerged at 5.20 p.m.
there he was, with a ramshackle old car and a shifty-looking
driver.

'Overslept a bit after all that exertion, did you?' he asked with
a conspiratorial wink. 'Hop in.'

There were no taxis around and there was no avoiding it.

The Castillo San Miguel was standing in much its present
form and in its present commanding position on a low hill
slightly back from the coast, when Mings's fleet had presented
itself off Campeche. But, as we have seen, its guns could not
effectively cover the seaward approach to the town. This struck
us as strange, until we were told that the Spaniards had almost
certainly reckoned that any ships menacing Campeche would
approach by the channel parallel with the coast, either from the
north or from the south. Mings, by good seamanship, had

The gun terrace of the Castillo San Miguel at Campeche

arrived directly opposite the town before sailing in towards it; in so doing, by good luck he had avoided any of the reefs and shallows immediately off the town. When a few days later we flew over this stretch of coastline, this theory seemed even more likely to represent the truth: there were discolourations in the waters off the town which appeared to represent underwater hazards. Mings might well have been luckier than he realized, and the effect on Morgan could have been to make him overconfident in such circumstances – an overconfidence which was to cost him at least one of his flagships.

The walls and turrets of the Castillo had been well restored; the moat cleared; a selection of guns – mostly of a somewhat later period – placed on the battlements and artillery terraces. The rooms off the interior courtyard had been converted into a tidy but unexciting museum.

Mr Barraclough did not share our interest in these matters. He settled on a stone bench in the courtyard, for all the world like a grog-soaked buccaneer catching his breath after an exhausting assault, and eyed the other visitors to the castillo with a predatory gaze. Few escaped some denigratory comment, muttered in English on the confident assumption that it would pass over the heads of the locals.

'Twenty stone on the hoof,' he murmured ungallantly as a large Mexican matron climbed, panting heavily, the steps of the battlements.

'Clear case of ingrowing virginity,' he grumbled as a handsome young Mexican lady declined to return his leery smile.

When eventually we finished our tour of the castillo, Mr Barraclough homed on to us.

'Want to see the dungeons?' he proposed, in the tone of an Arab street vendor offering his sister. It turned out that the dungeons were either inaccessible or non-existent.

Pedro, owner of the dubious 'jalopy' in
Campeche

'You won't repeat that stuff about my being taken for the Consul, will you, old boy? You see, it might upset the Major.'

'The Major?' I enquired.

'Chap called Dutton. Very straight guy. He's Hon. Consul in Merida. Been there for years. Wouldn't like to upset him, specially as there's a slightly embarrassing little piece of business one of my associates has got himself into in that quarter.'

The use of the term 'one of my associates' seemed to restore his self-confidence. He bellowed for Pedro. There was no sign of Pedro nor of his jalopy.

'Must have had an urgent call. Busy chap, Pedro. Never mind. Tell you what: if you like to slip me a couple of hundred of the local piastres I'll settle up with him for the run out here next time I see him.'

Weakly, I started to take out my wallet.

'Second thoughts: better make it four hundred, old boy. You know what petrol's like these days.'

Morgan's second raiding expedition into New Spain – that of 1664 – was not under Mings's command. Indeed, he was under no one's command: Henry Morgan was one of five equal and independent young captains, the others being his friend John Morris, a Dutchman called David Marteen, and two others called Freeman and Jackman. They all had valid privateers' commissions signed by the Governor of Jamaica, Lord Windsor. They had chosen their crews, largely from among buccaneers with whom they had earlier sailed, and they had paid for the provisioning of their ships themselves, largely on borrowed money. After the success of the Santiago and the Campeche raids, the privateers' credit was good.

Unlike Mings's fleet, which had amounted to a total force of over a thousand men, the little squadron which sailed from Port Royal at the end of 1663 numbered less than two hundred men in all. Not for them the risks of an attack on a fortified coastal town: they would have to find a softer target – inland, unprepared, without defences. The problem about such targets was that they were, by definition, inaccessible. The young captains decided that, since this was so, they would do well to face the fact and choose the most inaccessible objective they could – an inland town, sixty miles up a river the mouth of which was thirteen hundred miles from Port Royal. Villahermosa, capital of the province of Tabasco in New Spain, was their unsuspecting goal.

Morgan and his associates rounded the Yucatán peninsula and sailed southwards down the coast to the latitude of Campeche, just as they had done with Mings the year before. After Campeche they had one navigational aid unavailable to Mings; they had left astern the limestone plateau of Yucatán and now, for the first time for 300 miles, there were rivers issuing into the sea as an indication of how far down the coast they had reached. First they passed the muddy mouth of the Rio Champotón, then the Rio Candelaria, then the Rio San Pedro and finally the Rio Grijalva. This was to be their channel of advance inland to Villahermosa.

Or so they thought. Across the mouth of the river lay a small sandy island, and careful navigation was necessary to circumvent this and start sailing up the river. They anchored, and the five captains disembarked with just over a hundred of their followers. Five miles up the river was the tiny settlement of Frontera, once the scene of the first landing by Cortes and the Conquistadors on their way to Veracruz, but now inhabited by Indians. As the buccaneers were so often to find, they were welcomed by the Indians, who had suffered so horribly under the cruelty of their Spanish masters that any enemy of the Dons was a friend of theirs. But the Indians had bad news for Morgan and his fellow captains: to approach Villahermosa up the river was to court disaster, as there was no way that a waterborne advance could be made undetected in advance by the Spaniards. Any secret approach must be made by a march overland.

But this was easier said than done. The land on both sides of the river Grijalva was far from solid. Not only did the river itself meander tortuously, but there was a patchwork of lakes, swamps and muddy waterways stretching far out from both banks. Men might wander indefinitely, on foot or in boats, in this quagmire; indeed, they might disappear forever without trace.

The Indians came to the rescue of the buccaneers: they would act as guides, provided the expedition was to be against the Spaniards, and provided the buccaneers did not mind a long march. The captains agreed, little realizing that when the Indians referred to a long march they were suggesting a route that would be more than five times the distance of the river route – a three-hundred-mile trek through swamp and jungle in the tropical temperatures of Tabasco, taking the buccaneers round the periphery of the region of lakes and avoiding all habitations from which news of their advance might leak back to the Spaniards at Villahermosa.

The strategy worked. When eventually the small, weary force of one hundred buccaneers came upon Villahermosa they surprised it completely. They captured not only the town, but three hundred prisoners and considerable booty. Laden with their spoils, they returned to the coast, this time by the direct and more comfortable route of the river. It was then that their real troubles started.

While the buccaneers had been marching painfully around the watery banks of the Grijalva, a squadron of Spanish coastal vessels, heavily armed, had put in at Frontera. The skeleton crews left on board the buccaneers' five ships were no match for the Spaniards: all the ships had been captured. Morgan and his men arrived back at the entrance to the river to find they had no means of making a getaway, let alone facing the thirteen-hundred-mile return voyage to Jamaica.

Happily they had not long to wait until some more Spanish shipping from Veracruz put in at Frontera. This time it was the buccaneers who had the advantage of numbers. Doubtless also the fact that they were stranded without stocks of provisions or ammunition on a hostile shore so far from home made them fight with more than usual desperation. At all events, two barques and four canoes were captured. These ships were poor replacements for their own more seaworthy vessels, but at least they enabled the buccaneers to continue their journey. The canoes were particularly heavy going; although they had some sort of jury-mast, most of the time they had to be propelled through these tropical seas by oarsmen. And the distances were daunting.

Slowly the little band of boats rounded the Yucatán peninsula and, hugging the coast, made their way down the Gulf of Honduras and as far south as the latitude of Nicaragua. Two more towns were attacked, and then it was time to turn due north-west and set a direct course for Port Royal.

Their arrival in Jamaica caused an instant crisis and necessitated the preparation of a full account of their exploits – the only contemporary one that exists – by the Governor. Much had changed in the twenty-two months that they had been away: not least, the Governor had changed. Lord Windsor had been replaced by Sir Thomas Modyford. Lord Windsor's commissions to privateers, including those to Morgan and his four fellow captains, had been cancelled. Peace had been signed with Spain. War had been declared on Holland. Lord Arlington – a Catholic and sympathizer with Spain – had been appointed as Secretary of State in London. At least one privateer – Captain Searle – had been forced to return his prizes to Spain. Another – Captain Munro – who had refused to countenance the cancellation of his commission, and who had continued as before, had been hung in chains at Gallows Point. Some fairly rapid and convincing explaining had to be done.

This Sir Thomas Modyford did. He was to be a friend and ally of Morgan throughout his career, and never more usefully so than on this occasion. He accepted the contention of the young captains that they had never been informed of the peace treaty. He addressed his report not to the Earl of Arlington but to the Duke of Albemarle who, as chairman of the Privy Council's committee for foreign plantations, was well disposed towards privateers who provided a cheap defence force for such outlying plantations as Jamaica. He drafted the report with skill and care, maintaining that the whole expedition might be viewed more as a reconnaissance than as an attack.

In consequence Morgan, Morris and the others were not only

reprieved but treated as heroes: not for them the fate of Searle or Munro. They were now rich men in their own right, able to command credit and raise recruits. And of none was this so true as of Henry Morgan. The Villahermosa expedition had made him *primus inter pares* among the buccaneers; his soldierly qualities on the long march and the short attack had proved decisive. The watery wastes around the River Grijalva were as essential a destination in the quest for Morgan as had been the walls and towers of Campeche.

Again, Caroline and I set out to explore the terrain from Merida. The season was high summer. Temperatures were consistently in the nineties, with humidity to match. The thought of the road journey to Villahermosa – far longer than to Campeche – was daunting: two days on a bus and little prospect of a first-class one being available. Moreover, when we got to Villahermosa we should find we were out of the frying pan into the fire. Graham Greene, who even in 1938 had been no stranger to the steamier parts of the earth, wrote in *The Lawless Roads*, 'to know how hot the world can be I had to wait for Villahermosa'.

Another problem was that the real interest for us was not the town itself. In Villahermosa, unlike Campeche, nothing of importance was left of the seventeenth-century buildings. The significant thing for us was the surrounding countryside – those hundreds of square miles of lake, swamp and jungle round and through which Morgan and his men had been led by the Indians between Frontera and their objective. What was the country really like? Was it the watery labyrinth that it had been portrayed as being? Which side of the river had the Indians taken him: east or west? What was the River Grijalva like between the sea and Frontera? And was the approach to the mouth of the river really as tricky as described? These were questions which no bus journey from Merida to Villahermosa could answer. It was a problem.

Perhaps it was the obvious awe with which Mr Barraclough had spoken of 'the Major' that made me feel I should pay my respects to the genuine Honorary Consul. Or perhaps it was a nudge from St Christopher or whatever kindly genius presides over perversely persistent travellers. Whatever the reason, I put on a clean shirt, walked two blocks down the road from our hotel and called on the office of Major A. Dutton, MBE.

Major Dutton's father had arrived in Merida in 1906 to provide and maintain machinery for the sisal industry. The family established a name for engineering skills and probity going far beyond the confines of Yucatán. They had bought the solidest house in the solidest street in Merida; they had put down roots – while not being too preoccupied to return to Europe to fight for their home country when she needed them; they were pillars of the local yacht club at Progreso. Best of all, they had bought an aeroplane: a four-seater single-engined Cessna.

Major Dutton had a much better idea than committing us to a two-day bus ride to Villahermosa. He had business himself in Chiapas and Tabasco which required attention in the next few days. Would we not like to see the famed Mayan ruins of Palenche? If so, he could fly us down there and leave us for a day or two while he did his business, and then on his return journey pick us up and – who knows – possibly if time permitted overfly the surroundings of Villahermosa, and retrace the route of the Grijalva river to the coast. We had a curious sensation of echoing Graham Greene's experience in *The Lawless Roads* with regard to Palenche. He had written: 'I had set myself two jobs – to get to Villahermosa and to cross Chiapas; Palenche was only a side issue, a blind for officials, and now suddenly I found it taking possession of my route – I was being driven like a sheep through a gate.'

But we were very content to be driven through this particular gate. Firstly, Palenche was on the edge of the country we wished to explore: the jungle which enveloped the ruins was the same forested country which stretched into Tabasco and up to Villahermosa. Secondly, there was always the possibility that the Major might be prepared to made a diversion for us over the Grijalva river and the swamps through which Morgan had struggled. Besides, to have been to Chiapas, or even Tabasco, and not to have seen the ruins of Palenche would have been like missing the chance to see Uxmal on the way to Campeche – worse, in fact.

What differentiates Palenche from the more developed and frequented Yucatán sites of Chichen Itza and Uxmal is the fact that Palenche still peers at the visitor out of its natural jungle setting. The Temple of the Inscriptions has a backcloth of forest-clad hillside; the Temple of the Sun looks down on a trilling mountain stream; a waterfall flanks the ruins. Because of this intervention of nature one feels a sense of discovery at every fresh monument encountered.

But still we experienced the same 'non-recognition' as at Uxmal: the sense of being unable to relate. One of the most colourful of the pioneer archaeologists of Palenche, a certain Count Frederik de Waldek, was clearly bothered by the same sensation, so he set about 'manufacturing' links with the cultures of ancient Egypt and other more comprehensible civilizations. For two years, in the 1830s, Count de Waldek lived in one of the temples at Palenche with his lady friend, always unearthing fresh ruins and usually doing a little 'tidying up' of the evidence to fit his theories. When his work was finally published he was already aged 100, and was to live for a further happy nine years during which no one had the temerity to question his findings and theories.

We found a hotel near the ruins and spent much of our first day clambering over them. Walking down the hill past the waterfall in the evening, we fell into conversation with a man who was leading a string of mules which he had been watering at the river. We had it on our consciences that flying over the country around Villahermosa would not be quite the same as experiencing it for ourselves, directly and on the ground. We therefore asked the muleteer if we could hire two of his mules for the following day. He said we could if we hired him and a third mule too. Where did we want to go? I explained that we wanted to head towards Villahermosa, but avoiding the road, to get some idea of the countryside. He looked at us as if he doubted whether we were mentally stable enough to be entrusted with his mules. When later, in answer to a question, we told him we were British, he nodded understandingly as if this explained a great deal, and agreed to set off with us at six o'clock the next morning. In this way, he said, he hoped we would be among the trees by the time the sun got up.

The muleteer encountered at Palenche in the Chiapas region of Mexico

It was a vain hope. By 9 a.m. the sun was blazing down on us as we crossed a green, rolling countryside, interspersed with patches of cultivation. We were on a bearing north-west from Palenche heading towards the village of Salto de Agua. The mules were soon at their old trick of hanging back unless goaded on with cries of 'Mula, mula!', prods from sticks and kicks with heels. We asked the muleteer if there were still any 'tigers' (leopards) in Chiapas, and he said he had heard of people encountering them. Were we hunters? When we explained that we were not, that we merely were interested in covering ground over which a compatriot had travelled three hundred years ago, only his good manners prevented him from displaying his incredulity. When eventually we reached a more forested region and saw signs of recent tree-felling, we asked him about the uses of the local timber. He replied by asking us whether we wanted to buy a tract of local land for development? There must be some reason better than the one we had given for enduring this discomfort, surely?

By midday we were sore and stiff, thirsty and hot, but not quite as desperate as Graham Greene had become on this same journey. Unlike him, we had ridden mules before, and also unlike him I wore a light Panama hat rather than a heavy helmet which 'was just the damp hot cardboard it pretended not to be'. We drank from our water-bottles and ate some sandwiches beside the path, giving some to our muleteer as he appeared not to have brought any food – probably on the assumption that we would have abandoned our project before he had time to get hungry.

We had been following a well-marked track that gradually deteriorated into wetter and swampier ground. The mules were making ever heavier going of it, faltering and hesitating. Ahead it looked even marshier. We might have persisted into the swamps for a while, at least to see the effect on our rate of progress of plodding through the squelching, muddy undergrowth. I was anxious to work out a time/distance ratio for the routes which Morgan might have taken on his march with the Indians. But fate intervened in the shape of a small field-mouse.

Being a sensible creature, the mouse in question was inhabiting a small island of solid ground amid the surrounding liquid. It ran along the top of a fallen tree trunk, perched at the end of it and contemplated the oncoming mules and riders. The mouse saw Caroline, and Caroline saw the mouse. Neither appeared unduly moved by the experience. (Caroline's attitude towards field-mice is – at best – ambivalent: there was a moment in our early married life when I came to her rescue by trapping one under a waste paper basket in the bathroom of our house in England, only to be told five minutes later that the poor mouse might be frightened of the dark and that I ought to release it.)

The trouble began when this Mexican mouse disappeared down a hole; the odd thing being that it was not the mouse that went into the hole, but the hole that engulfed the mouse. It was not only Caroline's instincts for the prevention of cruelty to mice that were aroused, but her lively horror also, when she observed that the black hole down which it had disappeared was in fact the open mouth of a large snake.

There is nothing ambivalent about Caroline's attitude to carnivorous snakes. She started up in her saddle as if bitten. Her mule, doubtless sensing her alarm, reacted in the unhelpful way in which mules usually respond to an emergency: it shied and lashed out with its back legs. Caroline, caught off balance, landed on the ground three feet from the snake.

I had always thought that the hissing of serpents was one of those subjective sounds, like the whispering of the wind and the clicking of Prussian heels, which were literary rather than auditory experiences. I was disabused: hiss was what this snake quite audibly did.

Our muleteer's reaction (he was the last of the three of us to see the menacing coil of green and yellow) was to throw the stick, with which he had been prodding and thrashing his mule, straight at the snake. I could have thought of nothing more calculated to enrage the already disconcerted reptile. The stick fell – with a rustle of leaves – a yard from the hissing head. I suppose the snake thought it was being menaced from a new quarter; the sharp eyes and sharper fangs turned, and in that

second Caroline was on her feet and with a single leap some
further six feet away.

From then on, everyone seemed to be fleeing from something
else. Caroline ran fleet-footed from the snake; the snake squiggled away from the general hubbub, presumably contracting
severe indigestion on account of the newly-swallowed mouse;
the mules pranced off – heels flaying the air – away from where
the snake had been. It was a full ten minutes before we had all
reassembled and collected ourselves.

Our momentum had been checked. Although we were still a
long way from the immediate surroundings of Villahermosa, we
had seen for ourselves the quality of the problems that the
terrain presented. All that remained was to get an idea of the
quantity; that we could only do from the air, on the morrow.

The next morning Major Dutton collected us in the Cessna at
the airstrip. We waited for him in an open hut which constituted virtually the only airport building. One wall was covered
with a political poster publicizing the candidate for Chiapas in
some election; he appeared full-face and profile, scowling under
his heavy moustache, as in a police 'Wanted' poster. As we
prepared for take-off we observed, in the nick of time, a small
child who was playing idly under the wheel of the Cessna. His
unconcerned father appeared to resent our spoiling his son's fun
by wishing to take off.

As soon as we were in the air, Major Dutton turned the little
plane away from the hills and towards the more open country
which we had traversed the day before. Soon the rolling
greenery and the patches of forest were giving way to wetter and
flatter country as we approached Villahermosa. The morning
sun glittered on sheet after sheet of water – some of them muddy
brown, some inky black, some covered in brilliant green weed.
As we got nearer to Villahermosa the sinuous blue bends of the
Grijalva added yet another shape and colour to the dappled
landscape beneath us. There was frequently more water than
land.

We circled Villahermosa and, as we expected, saw no trace of

The watery banks of the river Grijalva as seen from Major Dutton's
Cessna

seventeenth-century structures. Cemeteries, walled courtyards, police stations . . . these we did see, and wondered
whether any of them might have been the putative scene of the
final adventures and execution of Graham Greene's whisky
priest. The town looked world-weary and hot even from a
thousand feet above.

After Villahermosa we followed the course of the Grijalva. It
was like an illustration in a child's atlas intended to explain the
meaning of the term 'meander' and to show the process of
erosion continually changing the course of a river. It snaked its
way through banks scarcely less liquid than itself, continually
almost short-circuiting itself.

This was the country round and through which his Indian
guides had led Morgan and his men on their march to surprise

the town. Never can guides have been more necessary: without them a body of men could wander interminably in these watery mazes. In the reports on Morgan's campaign it was never stated whether he went east or west of the Grijalva on his progress south from Frontera. We speculated on this point as we studied the ground from a thousand feet above and concluded that – unless the structure of the terrain (as opposed to the immediate course of the river) had changed fundamentally in the last three hundred years – it seemed certain that the Indians would have taken Morgan in a loop around the western side of the Grijalva.

Soon Frontera was below us: a patchwork of crisscrossed streets stuck on to the west bank of the river and looking as neat and tidy as a housing estate from this height. This had been the scene of Cortes's first landing in Mexico, but he had sailed on to Veracruz before attempting to penetrate inland; as we had seen, he had been right to do so. Was the ship alongside the wharf the *General Obregon*, we wondered, and where was Mr Trench's dental surgery? We were still in the heart of Greene-land.

From here it was only six miles to the open sea. A sandy island, the shape of a hook, lay across the mouth of the river, emphasizing once again the hazards which conquistadors and buccaneers alike had had to face in making a landfall at all along this stretch of coast.

This was the coast notorious for 'northers' – those storms, not of hurricane proportions but none the less of fierce force, which blew down from the north, forcing shipping on to the low sandbanks, the coral reefs or the inhospitable shore of the Bay of Campeche. The Spanish *flota* bringing the gold and silver plate from Veracruz to the rendezvous with the galleons from Cartagena at Havana had been particularly vulnerable to northers: more than a score of ships from the *flotas* had been wrecked on this Tabasco coast between 1563 and 1571 alone. Heavy losses had continued into the seventeenth century and the buccaneers were often even more at risk than the Spanish, since their ships were frequently – notably in the case of Morgan's 1664 expedition – less seaworthy. Some of the coastal vessels still looked remarkably small and frail, we thought, as we saw

Fishing boats at Carmen island, once a haunt of buccaneers and still
haunted by their descendents

them from the air inching down the coast. Graham Greene's
experience in sailing down from Veracruz to Frontera had
hardly been reassuring. He had been told that ships like the one
on which he was travelling did not often sink 'unless you hit a
norther'; and when he had suggested that the norther season
was over he had been told 'You can't tell. Anyway, they insure
you for five thousand pesos when you buy a ticket.'

From the mouth of the Grijalva we followed the coast
north-east for fifty miles until we reached the island of Carmen,
with the town of that name on its south-western extremity. The
island had been a haunt of buccaneers, though not particularly
of Morgan. However, Major Dutton thought the connection
was sufficient to warrant landing. We circled a lighthouse
which, we were told, was entirely faced in English bathroom
tiles, and landed at an airfield which could hardly have been
more different from Palenche: every few minutes giant helicop-

ters took off laden with crews for off-shore oil-rigs. 'Take no liquor. Hand in your firearms. Have a shower – travel clean' . . . a stark set of injunctions scrawled on a blackboard confronted the crews as they formed up to take their seats aboard.

The Major hailed a taxi. If we didn't mind getting involved with some present-day buccaneers, he suggested, we might like to come with him on a little trip – to find a ship and collect a bad debt. We set off through the bustling, oil-rich little town, soon making the transition from tarmac roads to gravel, and then from gravel to shingle. We travelled along a spit of land on which was parked a solitary, ramshackle car which looked not unlike Pedro's famed jalopy from Campeche; but then all old Fords look a bit alike. We were heading for a rusty hulk which, the Major explained, despite its appearance of being unlikely to weather the mildest norther, was now sporting a fully operational modern radar system, thanks to the services of his firm. There were certain little matters about the payment for these services which could no doubt be settled in a gentlemanly manner if the Major could just get the ear of the Master for a moment, we gathered.

There was no sign of life on board, but eventually a bedraggled hand appeared from the bowels of the ship. 'No, the Master was not aboard. No, he didn't know when he would be back. No, he didn't know where he had gone.' There was nothing for it but to turn on our heels and go back down the cat-walk to the shore. It was strange how the low rumble from the Master's cabin sounded almost like human voices . . . how the creaking of the gangplank sounded almost like laughter . . . how after we reached the shore the sea breeze wafted a single phrase – in an unforgotten English voice – to my ear: 'Near squeak, old boy . . . calls for a glass of the local poison!'

Who was it had said at the Beefsteak that night that the Caribbean still held its share of rascals?

4

Morgan's Venture to the Cuban Interior

It was in January 1668 that Henry Morgan made the transition from being one of the many brethren of the coast to being their leader. Governor Modyford was just as concerned as Lord Windsor had been before him by the Spanish threat to Jamaica: the Spaniards had recently recaptured the island of Old Providence (between Jamaica and the Main), and their nearest harbours were only some hundred miles away on the Cuban coast. Modyford was feeling exposed. He was therefore prepared to issue letters of marque and encourage the collection of a fleet to harass the Spaniards in Cuba. To whom better could this task be entrusted than to the hero of the Villahermosa expedition?

Morgan needed little coaxing. This was the opportunity for which he had prepared himself. His share of the loot from the Villahermosa expedition was now invested in two barques of his own. In company with his friend Captain Morris (also now the proud owner of his own barque) he sailed from Port Royal to a prearranged rendezvous at one of the small cays off the southern coast of Cuba, possibly in the San Felipe group. Here he was joined by nine other small ships, some being manned by French buccaneers from Tortuga. The total fighting force amounted to around 700 men, of whom probably about 450 were English (with a sprinkling of Welsh and Scots); with a fleet of this composition, there was little inclination to challenge Morgan's overall command. But command did not imply the right to impose operational conditions or even objectives on the expedition.

Long before this date, the brethren of the coast had established their own rules of operation and their own code of conduct, which was broadly democratic and in many respects surprisingly sophisticated. The buccaneers chose their own captains and – as they began to operate in larger fleets – their own 'Admiral of the Brethren'. Indeed, it was the death of Edward Mansfield, the former admiral, that induced Modyford to place Morgan in overall command in recognition of his emergence as the obvious successor.

The way in which the buccaneers reached their decisions, and how they lived, are best described by a Dutchman called Esquemeling, whom Morgan first met at the council of war in January 1668, and who was to become the principal chronicler of Morgan's expeditions. Esquemeling makes the whole process sound like a well-organized shooting expedition.

To start with, a precise embarkation date was announced 'intimating also to them their obligation to bring each man in particular so many rounds of powder and bullets as they think necessary for that expedition'. Then as soon as the buccaneers had assembled they would hold a council to decide 'what place they ought first to go to wherein to get provisions – especially of flesh, seeing they scarce eat anything else'. Tortoise meat was apparently a particular favourite, but pork was the staple diet. They would therefore plan night raids on Spanish hog-yards, intimidating or killing the swineherds. A lot of meat had to be stolen and salted, because the buccaneers did not believe in stinting themselves while on an operation:

> Their allowance (of flesh), twice a day to every one, is as much as he can eat, without either weight or measure. Neither does the steward of the vessel give any greater proportion of flesh or anything else to the captain than to the meanest mariner.

Once they were armed and provisioned, the buccaneers would call another council to decide on the target for their attack. At this meeting they would also decide upon and sign certain written articles setting out the financial conditions of the venture. The fundamental principle was, of course, 'No purchase, no pay'. But assuming there would be considerable 'purchase' or loot to be divided, they had to settle in advance the manner in which this would be shared. There would be fixed salaries for the ship's carpenter and for the ship's surgeon, who would be expected to fit himself out with an adequate medicine chest before sailing. Then there would be a scale of compensation to be agreed for those who might be wounded on the exploit. These rates compared very favourably with those offered in the Royal Navy a century and a half later. Examples of compensation were 'for the loss of a right arm, six hundred pieces of eight or six slaves; for the loss of a left arm, five hundred pieces of eight or five slaves'. (Buccaneers were assumed to be right-handed.) Curiously, the loss of an eye rated no more than the loss of a finger – one hundred pieces of eight or one slave. Lastly they would settle the proportions in which the remaining 'purchase' was to be split up between the participants; customarily the captain would be allotted six portions, the mate two, the ordinary buccaneers one, and the ship's boys a half. (These last had to work hard for their money because they were expected to set fire to any vessels which the buccaneers abandoned after they had captured better ones: a dangerous task.)

Apparently there was some honour among thieves. For instance, Esquemeling reports that

> in the prizes they take, it is severely prohibited to every one to usurp anything in particular to themselves . . . Yea, they take a solemn oath to each other not to abscond, or conceal the least thing they find among the prey. If afterwards any one is found unfaithful, who has contravened the said oath, immediately he is separated and turned out of the society. Among themselves they are very civil and charitable to each other. In so much that if any wants what another has, with great liberality they give it one to another.

One wonders. The vision of the rank and file of the rough and ready brethren of the coast agreeing elaborate terms of contract is a little hard to conjure up. Even more so is the good-natured handing over by one shipmate to another of a cherished pistol, amulet or ring. But one thing is certain: the buccaneers had a *modus operandi* of their own which blended some features of disreputable piracy with others of more fastidious privateering.

Esquemeling is the source for so much of what we know about the practices of the buccaneers, that it is worth looking closely at the man. Alexander Olivier Esquemeling – variously spelt Exquemelin or even Oexmelin – was a Dutch physician who was to spend six years with Morgan and the buccaneers and subsequently write a racy account of their exploits, which was first published in Holland and later in England, France and Spain. Because he was an eyewitness to many of the major incidents (though probably not to as many as he claimed) he is a major source for any work on Morgan, but not a necessarily accurate source. For one thing, he is prone to exaggeration: the height of mountains, the numbers of opponents, the gravity of wounds – all lose nothing in the telling. Another failing is that he tends to be vague about the tactics of military engagements, perhaps because as a doctor he did not understand what was going on, or perhaps because he kept himself a prudent distance from the action. A more important failing is his prejudice: Esquemeling had repented of his buccaneering days before he came to write his history, and he is at pains to express disapproval of all barbarities and even to exaggerate these in his efforts to distance himself from them. There is a sanctimonious flavour to the commentary which goes ill with the full-blooded nature of the narrative. In addition, he had fallen out with Morgan (possibly over the distribution of the 'purchase' after the Panama raid) and seldom misses a chance to malign his former leader. For these reasons, when his book eventually reached Jamaica from England, Morgan sued for damages. But all this was a long way in the future when the young Dutchman sailed in on one of the French ships from Tortuga and joined the embryonic expedition in January 1668.

Esquemeling gives a detailed account of the deliberations at the council of war. Havana appealed as a target to many of the buccaneers, and some of them argued that a night assault would be 'convenient'; indeed, they maintained that such an enterprise might easily be performed 'if they could but take a few of the ecclesiastics and make them prisoners'. With the help of such hostages, the cover of darkness and total surprise it was hoped that the city might be sacked before the castles could put themselves in a posture of defence.

More cautious counsels prevailed. A number of the buccaneers had already been held prisoner by the Spaniards in Havana and had no enthusiasm for repeating the experience. These men persuaded the others that it would be madness to attempt the attack with a force of less than 1,500 men. It was proposed by one of those present – Esquemeling does not say by whom – that an overland attack on Havana, after a march across the island from the south coast, might stand the best chance of success. (The same thought was to occur to those who planned the invasion at the Bay of Pigs almost exactly three centuries later.) It may have been Morgan who put forward this plan: many of his later successful assaults were to involve land attacks from an unexpected quarter. Indeed, with the authority and self-confidence that he was to achieve later, he might have carried the day in favour of attacking the rich prize of Havana. As it was, he allowed himself to be persuaded – in the 'democratic' manner of the buccaneers – that Puerto Principe would be a more realistic objective.

One of the attractions for the buccaneers of the town of Puerto Principe was that it had never been attacked before, and might therefore be assumed to have accumulated considerable riches. It was reported that the inhabitants were wealthy and 'exercised their trade for ready money' with the merchants of Havana. The trade was based on hides. In fact, had they but known it, Puerto Principe was a centre of no special significance or opulence; it consisted of no more than a hundred houses; its mundane inhabitants used salted meat and eggs rather than silver as the medium of exchange. Even the name was misleading: Puerto Principe was forty miles inland. Its former residents, having tired of being regularly ravaged by pirates, had moved their town away from the coast while preserving the original name.

Having reached his decision to attack Puerto Principe, Morgan rather surprisingly did not immediately sail in that direction. Instead, he rounded the western end of Cuba and paraded his fleet off the Morro at Havana. Historians have disagreed about his motives for this. Some have argued that it was bravado; others that he was attempting to cause a diversion and mislead the Spaniards about the destination of his expedition. It seems more likely, however, that he was fulfilling – at least in ritual form – Modyford's injunctions to give the Spaniards a sharp warning. In this he succeeded: the governor and garrison of Havana feverishly set about reinforcing their entrenchments. Spanish energies were deflected to the defensive.

His gesture made, Morgan turned his ships' bows towards the west, rounded the point of Cuba once more, and eventually anchored in the bay of Santa Maria, about half way along the southern coast. This was the nearest point to Puerto Principe. Here a serious setback occurred. A Spanish prisoner, who had been picked up on one of the cays and who was not thought to understand English, had overheard and understood the buccaneers making their plans. As soon as the ships anchored, he managed to dive overboard, swim ashore, and carry the news to the Spanish settlers in the interior.

The governor of Puerto Principe, no doubt deploring the fact that his citizens had not moved their town even further inland, wasted no time in preparing for Morgan's party. What few valuables the inhabitants possessed were quickly removed to places of hiding. In a short space of time he managed to assemble a remarkably numerous defence force considering the size of the town. In addition to the Spanish militia, he conscripted slaves from the neighbouring estates; in all, he managed to muster some 800 men – a hundred more than the total number of his assailants. The governor also had the few established paths between the coast and the town blocked with trees felled for the purpose. He then arranged ambushes on the tracks which the buccaneers would be likely to take to avoid the blocked paths. Finally, he arranged to deploy the main body of his force in the open country in front of the town, where the enemy could be confronted, outnumbered and repulsed before they ever managed to enter the town precincts. In short, he made good use of the advance warning given him by the escaped prisoner.

Esquemeling is disappointingly uninformative about the details of the buccaneers' approach march. He tells us that they found the blocked paths 'impenetrable', and that they consequently took to the forests, where they encountered 'great difficulty' and narrowly escaped from 'divers ambuscades'. He does not even report how long the march took. We can only conjecture that the first part of the route must have been swampy, the middle section densely wooded, and the final approach across savannah country. The battle that ensued on the plain in front of the town lasted four hours; it was a hard-fought contest. Esquemeling, who labels the buccaneers as pirates rather than privateers, is more precise than usual in describing the course of the battle:

> The Governor, seeing them come, made a detachment of a troop of horse, which he sent to charge them in the front, thinking to disperse them, and, by putting them to flight, pursue them with his main body. But this design succeeded not as it was intended. For the Pirates marched in very good rank and file, at the sound of their drums and with flying colours. When they came near the horse, they drew into the form of a semicircle, and thus advanced towards the Spaniards, who charged them like valiant and courageous soldiers for some while. But seeing the Pirates were very dextrous at their arms, and their Governor, with many of their companions, killed, they began to retreat towards the wood. Here they designed to save themselves with more advantage; but, before they could reach it, the greatest part of them were unfortunately killed.

The buccaneers, who had sustained only very slight casualties, immediately set about entering the town, where they were met by sniping and resistance in the streets and houses. While they had been prepared to engage in battle on the plain, they were not prepared to suffer losses while they set about the pillaging for which they had come. An ultimatum was therefore issued to the inhabitants: either they surrendered immediately, or the town would be set alight and their wives and children 'torn in pieces'. In these circumstances, the townsfolk submitted.

For the first time in his career, Morgan found himself in overall command of a conquering force, with his opponents entirely at his mercy. He showed himself – as he was to do consistently thereafter – either unwilling or unable to impose the discipline in victory which he had managed to impose during the campaign and the fighting. He also conspicuously lacked compassion towards the vanquished.

No sooner had the Spaniards surrendered, than the buccaneers rounded them up – men, women, children and slaves – and locked them in the churches. They then set about the serious business of looting the town and pillaging the surrounding countryside. At first, a good many provisions were forthcoming. They fell to carousing among themselves, while allowing the prisoners to starve in the churches; Esquemeling records that many of the weaker captives – including children – perished during their incarceration.

When they failed to find more booty, the buccaneers turned to torturing the prisoners to induce them to tell where they had hidden their valuables during the period of preparation for the assault on their town. Before long they had exhausted this source of supply too. Morgan then decided that the best prospect of further income lay in persuading the prisoners to get neighbouring Spanish communities to pay a ransom for their release. If no such ransom were forthcoming, Morgan threatened to carry off the prisoners as slaves to Jamaica, and to reduce the town of Puerto Principe to ashes.

In the face of these threats, the Spanish prisoners elected

four of their own number to act as negotiators on their behalf. Morgan decided that it would increase their zeal in ransom-hunting if he tortured several of the prisoners to be left behind in the presence of the emissaries. Thus provided with fresh horrors to relate, the four spokesmen were set loose to raise the bullion which had been so singularly lacking in the houses and hideaways of the merchants of Puerto Principe.

After a few days, the emissaries returned to Morgan, to report that they had not been able to make contact with their compatriots, but that they were confident of being able to find them and raise the required ransom money if they were given another two weeks at liberty. Morgan was inclined to acquiesce in this, until one of his patrols returned from a scavenging expedition with a negro captive who had letters on him from the Spanish governor of Santiago de Cuba. When Morgan perused the letters he found that they were addressed to his prisoners, and that they were advising the prisoners to 'make not too much haste to pay any ransom for their town or persons' because the governor was on his way with a relief force to come to their rescue. The emissaries' plea for more time was thus revealed as a temporizing ploy.

Morgan promptly revised his plans. First, he told his prisoners that he could grant them no more time to find their ransoms. When this produced no more coin or bullion, he said he would accept payment in provisions: five hundred oxen or cows together with enough salt to preserve their meat. Furthermore, he insisted that the cattle should be delivered to his ships at their anchorage in the bay of Santa Maria, and that the butchering and salting should be done by the prisoners on the beach. To ensure delivery, Morgan took six of the principal prisoners as hostages with him and then decamped with his full force, and whatever booty they had been able to collect, to the coast. Although much encumbered, the buccaneers must have found the return march easier without the continual harassment of the ambuscades.

The prisoners released now seemed to encounter less difficulty in contacting their compatriots. Very rapidly they assembled the requisite herds, drove them to the coast, slaughtered them on the shore, and assisted with the loading of the buccaneers' barques. Morgan set free his six hostages, raised sail and made for a small island off the south-west of Hispaniola, where he set about dividing up the spoils of the adventure. (The island in question was to become a favourite rendezvous and haunt of Morgan's: the Spanish knew it as the Isla de Vacas, the French as the Ile à Vache, and the English anglicized it uncompromisingly as the Isle of Ash.)

The spoils were disappointing – 50,000 pieces of eight in all. In consequence, the French buccaneers decided to withdraw from the expedition and retired to their customary retreat of Tortuga. Their morale had been further lowered by an incident on the beach at Santa Maria, when an English sailor had got into a quarrel with one of the Frenchmen about some marrow bones from one of the slaughtered animals, and had 'drawn his sword treacherously against the Frenchman, wounding him in the back, before he had put himself in a just posture of defence; whereby he suddenly fell dead upon the place'. The other Frenchmen had been incensed. By placing the culprit in irons, and promising that he would be brought to trial on return to Jamaica, Morgan averted an ugly fracas on the beach; but the incident rankled and added to the grievances of the French contingent.

Historical evidence disagrees as to whether Morgan, now deserted by his French allies, returned directly to Jamaica or delayed in the cays south of Cuba until sufficiently reinforced to undertake his next expedition – against Portobello. Esquemeling is ambiguous on the point. Both the fact that many of the buccaneers had not earned a large enough share of the loot to pay their debts at home, and the fact that Morgan did not submit his report on the exploit until after his subsequent expedition to Portobello, suggest that there was no return to Port Royal between the two. On the other hand, Esquemeling reports that Morgan had the quarrelsome beach-fighter hanged promptly on his return to Jamaica, and it seems improbable that

that unfortunate man should have been held in irons throughout the Portobello campaign.

Be that as it may, when Morgan did get round to writing his
report to Modyford on the events in Cuba, he was at pains to
point out that he had taught the Spaniards a sharp lesson and
had secured Jamaica against attack. He even claimed that:

> We found that seventy men had been pressed to go against
> Jamaica, and that the like levy had been made in all the
> island, and that considerable forces were expected to rendez-
> vous at St Jago (Santiago) in Cuba.

Although Morgan's report linked the expeditions againt
Puerto Principe and Portobello, the former stands alone as a
campaign, and it was over when he made the division of the
spoils and parted with the French buccaneers at the Ile à Vache.
It can thus be assessed alone.

The Puerto Principe expedition had set a pattern which was
to be repeated in many of his subsequent adventures. It had
been undertaken ostensibly as a defensive operation against
Spanish imperialism in the Caribbean. The target had been
selected for motives of personal greed – in this case, rather
carelessly selected. The main achievement had been military
rather than naval: the serious fighting had been done on land.
Though the force was a loosely knit international one, discipline
and cohesion had been maintained, at least for the period of the
operations. Lastly – and most significantly and tragically – new
standards of barbarism had been allowed to characterize a
British military venture.

Morgan has often been compared with his illustrious predecessors on the Spanish Main, particularly Drake and Raleigh.
In many respects he stands up to the comparison. His grasp of
the strategic principles of surprise was as great as theirs, and his
ability to see enterprises in terms of combined sea and land
operations was as pronounced. The size of the forces under his
command bore comparison with theirs. Above all, the sheer
boldness and effrontery of his undertakings was in the tradition

of the finest Elizabethan exploits. But here the similarities end.

The differences are even more striking. Morgan did not have the long-range logistical problems of the Elizabethans: he had a secure and relatively nearby haven in Jamaica. Drake and Raleigh were both motivated by sentiments of patriotism in which their own ambitions were subsumed. Additionally, in the case of Drake, Protestant piety – in the face of the Spanish Inquisition at its cruellest and most uncompromising – played a central part in his make-up; in the case of Raleigh, a paternalism towards the Indians of Guyana foreshadowed the imperial vision of his countrymen in the centuries ahead. Both were cultivated men, despite their simple origins: Drake was an expert navigator; Raleigh a poet and historian. Morgan, on the other hand, seems always to have been motivated largely by avarice. His commissions for Modyford – as in Cuba – were technically fulfilled in the national interest, but always it was his own interests which dictated the manner of their fulfilment. The piety of Drake and the imaginative vision of Raleigh found no place in his character, where debauchery and grossness were too often their substitutes. Even if much of Esquemeling's censure is discounted – as it must be, since he was writing with the unctuous tone of one who had abandoned his former bad ways – the exploits of Morgan still have too many grisly episodes to be dismissed. Morgan made the alien religion of the Spaniards, and their notorious cruelty both to natives and captives, pretexts for even worse enormities of his own. But for all this the exploit of Puerto Principe was to fire the imagination of men of spirit throughout the Caribbean; it was to be the beginning of that legend of Captain Morgan that was to echo down the side corridors of history whenever deeds of daring at sea and on land are recounted.

[5]

A Later Venture to the Cuban Interior

Morgan had marched from the Bay of Santa Maria to Puerto Principe and back. From the outset, I resolved to cheat slightly: I would march from Puerto Principe to Santa Maria and back. To have done otherwise would have involved landing on a stretch of uninhabited, lonely coastline which would have aroused every instinct of mistrust in my Cuban hosts. It would be hard enough to organize the march from the Puerto Principe end.

The first problem was to find Puerto Principe. No such town exists in Cuba today, but some elementary research revealed that it is still there, but renamed Camaguey. The next problem was how to cover the ground: forty miles each way over a variety of terrain – agricultural land on the approaches to Camaguey, *manigua* (rough, wooded scrubland) between cultivation and the coastal strip, and mangrove swamp near the shore.

I discussed my project over dinner one night with one of the senior people in the Central Bank of Cuba, a charming and civilized man whose advice on local problems I had come to value.

'One advantage of being a banker in any country – communist or capitalist – is that a variety of people become indebted to you and are prepared to do you favours. Particularly farmers. Now if you should decide that you wanted to ride on this trip of yours,' he said, 'I just might be able to put you in touch with a farmer who could produce horses in the Camaguey region. Anyhow, let me know.'

Hiring reliable horses three hundred and fifty miles away from where you live (the distance between Camaguey and Havana) is not easy in any country. I had considered it would be impossible in Cuba. Now this offer opened new prospects. A few weeks later Caroline and I set off on an official visit to central Cuba, after which we decided to go on to Camaguey and the farm where – our friend told us – the horses were to be available. Our route took us through the Sierra de Escambray, that mountainous region where Castro's comrades, and later his opponents, had fought savage guerrilla campaigns. From the summit of the Sierra there is a steeply winding road leading down to the old colonial town of Trinidad, whose narrow cobbled streets, rickety wooden houses and crumbling bell-towers still provide a reminder of the Cuba which the Spanish had sought to defend against Morgan's incursions. This was the road we chose.

Other people's road accidents, like other people's operations, make boring stories. It is sufficient to say that our driver, while descending from the Sierra, experienced a total brake failure; the automatic gears on the heavy limousine also failed to hold. We lurched round hairpin bends on two wheels, an anti-kidnap siren screeching a warning to anyone unlucky enough to be coming in the other direction; eventually – just when we thought we could not take one more bend – the road levelled out and our speed reduced, but not enough to bring us to a halt. The road had a ditch and rock-face (contact with which would have invited instant conflagration) on one side, and a low parapet wall, protecting the road from a precipice, on the other. When our driver saw another bend approaching, with the prospect of further sharp descents, he did the most sensible thing: first, he crossed himself; then he methodically crashed the car in a series of sidelong bumps against the parapet wall. The parapet plunged into the landscape below, and our car and we ourselves sat battered and quivering on the edge. It was at that moment that I decided on the dedication of this book.

Rescue came. We reached Trinidad and booked in, shaken but thankful, at a hotel on the outskirts of the town, where the following day another car joined us. Meanwhile, a strong drink, a hot bath and early bed seemed indicated.

It was the second of these, the bath, which presented problems, or – to be more precise – it was the bathroom equipment. It was not that there was no bath plug: for that we were prepared with our flat, all-purpose rubber disk, without which we never ventured into the realms of alien plumbing. It was the tap. For some reason best known to the manufacturers of bathroom fittings the world over, there is a conspiracy against uniformity. The traditional twin taps, with their conventional spokes like miniature ships' helms, were long ago decreed to be too simple and the tap-makers of the world united to tease hotel bath users. First, they hit upon the perverse idea of mingling the water in one single nozzle, making it harder to control the temperature for the sake of mixing the hot and cold a fraction of a second earlier. Then they devoted their imagination and research resources to tampering with the taps: curious shapes were devised – levers, horns, dolphins, buttons . . . anything but the familiar twin helms. Our own bathroom in Trinidad had (in a rough translation of the hotel brochure) 'been equipped to a high standard of modernity'. This had resulted in the bath taps being reduced to a single chromium clutch, a curious phallic object like the joy-stick on an early aeroplane. Up and down, right and left it could be moved, to control volume and temperature. Cautiously we moved it out of neutral and a large spider spluttered into the bath-tub, to be followed by a sinister hiss of steam. We reverted to neutral and began again. Next time a cascade of ice-cold water, emitted from a hidden shower nozzle in the ceiling, drenched us from above. There was no way, it seemed, that it could be warmed or diverted to the lower level. Eventually we concluded that to have expected both a modern tap-unit *and* hot running water had perhaps been over-optimistic.

The night was uneventful until dawn, when we were disturbed at first light by the noise of the chairs on our ground-floor bedroom terrace being pushed around the floor. First one way, then the other, the wicker chairs, sofa and tables were shoved and dragged, their feet grating shrilly against the concrete floor. Surely, we thought, the hotel staff must have scrubbed it, swept it, dusted it and rearranged it by now? But no, the incessant movement to and fro of protesting furniture just outside our door went on and on. They started at 5 a.m.; they were still at it at 7 a.m.

'I'll go and ask them to stop it,' I said eventually in exasperation.

'Better not,' said Caroline sleepily. 'It's probably their job and they'll get into trouble if they're not seen being busy.'

We slept fitfully until 8 a.m. By then the sun was well up, and I drew the curtains on the windows giving on to the terrace. A scene of devastation met my blinking gaze. The wicker furniture was dismembered, the stuffed cushions disembowelled . . . everywhere there was splintered wood, with fragments of foam-rubber and mangled strips of material. Had some hooligan gang from Trinidad descended during the night? While Caroline and I stood staring in bewilderment and wondering if we would be blamed for this wanton destruction, a cheerful Cuban voice hailed us in Spanish from across the lawn:

'Mind out for the dogs!'

Dogs? We saw no dogs. Then the Cuban who had spoken to us came over to explain that packs of wild dogs frequented these parts at night and, by the look of our terrace, had been more than usually active in the past few hours.

'Just as well you didn't interrupt them,' said our informant. 'They can be very mean when they're disturbed.'

I looked at the mangled strips of material. I *supposed* they had been chair covers. They looked horribly like the remnants of a cotton print dress to me . . .

The following night was spent at Camaguey. Again, we were roused early; but this time because we had a rendezvous at dawn the next day at a Cuban state farm well beyond the southern outskirts of the town.

It was a strange encounter in the half-light. We had found the farm with difficulty and could just make out a line of horses tethered to a wooden rail beside a low wooden farmhouse. A dead dog was strung up in a tree at the gate of the farm (as a warning of what, and to whom, one wondered), and a few – more fortunate ones – barked at our approach. The air was

Rafael, our guide through the mangrove swamps to the bay of Santa
Maria in Cuba

sweet with the smell of the tropics before the day's heat has
begun. The head of the state farm met us at the doorway; his
face fell at the sight of Caroline.

'They did not say there would be a lady.' His Spanish had a
strong rural Cuban intonation. 'We have no European saddles
. . . it will take perhaps fifteen hours riding to reach the Bay of
Santa Maria and get back . . . there is nowhere for a lady to stay
. . . women do not go into the *manigua* . . .'

'Then I'll stay here,' said Caroline. 'It looks as if there are
lovely walks around, and I've got a good book to read. Don't
worry about me.'

We all sat round a scrubbed trestle-table and fortified
ourselves for the long ride ahead with a substantial breakfast:
eggs *revueltos* (broken fried eggs rather than properly scrambled

ones), black bread, slices of garlic sausage and a nip of rum.

'The chestnut gelding looks a fine horse,' said Caroline. 'Would anyone mind if I just rode it round the farm for a minute while everyone's finishing breakfast?'

'It's the best horse this side of the Sierra,' said Rafael, a good-looking middle-aged farmhand who – I had been told – was to be my self-appointed escort and guide. 'Takes a bit of handling, though.'

'Let her try,' I suggested.

Caroline mounted without assistance, took the horse in a controlled canter round what might – in other circumstances – have been called a paddock, jumped a small stream, dismounted deftly and tethered the horse professionally to the rail.

'I haven't seen a better horse the other side of the Sierra either,' she said. 'But surely it's time you were both on your way?'

There was a general movement of preparation: saddle-bags were strapped on horses; water bottles were filled; Rafael slung a rifle over his shoulder and stropped a machete on a grinding stone. Just as it seemed that Rafael and I were about to mount, the head man came up to me in a faintly confidential way.

'The lady rides like a boy, not like a woman. Rafael says he would be happy with her on one of his horses. We were not right to tell you that women never went into the *manigua* . . . there were Cuban women during the revolution who . . . ,' he trailed off.

'You mean Carolina can come?'

When I passed on the news Caroline's reaction was to slip a bottle of whisky from the glove-compartment of the car into a saddle-bag: 'Something tells me we're going to need this before we get back here,' she said.

There was to be no more cantering. The three of us set off at a steady gait across flat, open, grazing country. It was somewhere here – probably behind us and considerably closer to Camaguey/Puerto Principe – that the Spanish governor had drawn up his militia to confront the buccaneers, who at this point were marching in the 'very good rank and file' described by Esquemeling. It was an uncompromising countryside for a battle: no contours, no dead ground, no scope for anything but a straight slogging match: which was what took place.

Rafael told us that for him an expedition back to Santa Maria was a sentimental journey: he had only twice before in his life ventured into the *manigua* and the mangrove swamps around the Bay of Santa Maria and both times had been memorable.

The first time had been during the Cuban revolution. Fidel Castro, who was operating with his guerrillas in the Sierra Maestra mountains at the extreme eastern end of the island, decided in August 1958 to send two of his lieutenants – Camilo Cienfuegos and Che Guevara – westwards; they were to cut Batista's communications between Havana (in the west) and Santiago (in the east) and to link up with the rebel movement in the Sierra de Escambray (in the centre of the island). This involved Cienfuegos and Guevara, each with a few companions, separately crossing the province of Camaguey, which was firmly under Batista's control. The only safe way for these guerrilla leaders to travel was for them to keep far away from roads and villages, to march mostly by night, and to seek refuge in the *manigua*. Rafael had volunteered to be their guide. Cienfuegos and Guevara were no fair-weather soldiers, but even they found the going quite exceptionally tough. The former's report on this part of his campaign included a passage★ reading:

> During fifteen days we marched with no water and mud up to our knees, travelling by night to avoid ambushes . . . during the thirty-one days of our journey across Camaguey we ate eleven times. After four days of famine we had to eat a mare . . . Almost all our animals were left in the marsh.

The second occasion on which Rafael had traversed this region had been an even more traumatic experience for him. His ten-year-old son had gone on a hunting expedition with older boys into the *manigua* and they had not returned. After

★ Quoted by Professor Lord Thomas in his book *Cuba, or the Pursuit of Freedom* (London, 1971)

they had been missing for thirty-six hours Rafael had been desperate: he knew the dangers of getting lost in a region of swamps, alligators and no landmarks. For the first and only time in his life he had capitalized on his earlier heroic exploits: he had ridden into the nearest village where there was a telephone and after considerable difficulty got through to Che Guevara himself (by then a Minister in Castro's government).

Rafael disappears into the *manigua*

Within an hour helicopters were out from the Camaguey airforce base circling the area where the lost boys were thought to be. Units of the army arrived in trucks: a general search was on. Twelve hours later the boys were sighted from the air. Rafael rode in with an army officer who had radio contact with the helicopters, and rode out with his exhausted, frightened and starving child across the pommel of his saddle.

'Che was never one to forget his friends,' was Rafael's only comment on the incident.

By the time these stories had been narrated, we had covered some ten miles of open country: farm land had given way to savannah. And then, quite suddenly, a dark line across the middle distance announced the beginning of the *manigua*.

Riding through *manigua* is like riding through a blackberry bush several miles wide: everything gets torn – trousers, shirts, arms, cheeks. Rafael was concerned about Caroline. She was concerned about her horse. (No one was concerned about me.) The tangled greenery, enlivened by splashes of colour from passion-flowers, was strangely treacherous: velvety ferns were found to harbour rows of savage thorns on their reverse sides. Soon we came across a stream and rode down its course; the only drawback to this more comfortable method of progress was that every few hundred yards one of the horses and riders would stumble into a pot-hole on the bed of the stream and disappear up to the withers or the waist.

How had Morgan and his seven hundred men negotiated this terrain, I asked myself? The answer – almost certainly – was that they had not. In the seventeenth century this region had still been primary forest, with large trees and paths through it. Indeed, we know from Esquemeling that the governor of Puerto Principe had cut down trees to block the main thorough-fares and had laid ambushes on the diversionary tracks. The *manigua* with which we were coping was a secondary growth. For once, in retracing Morgan's footsteps, we were undertaking something harder than he had been called upon to do.

We knew from the compass that we were on a direct bearing for the Bay of Santa Maria, and we knew from the map that at some point on our line of advance the scrub would give way to mangrove swamp. When this occurred, instead of squelching steadily under foot, the horses began to trip over roots. The undergrowth was less thick but the water was no longer confined to the bed of the stream: it stretched like a brown liquid film around us.

'These roots aren't safe for the horses. One of them could break a leg,' said Rafael. 'The best thing we can do now is find a patch of higher ground and tether them, while we go ahead on foot.'

Finding the patch of higher ground proved easier said than done. Eventually we located a small island of relatively dry land amid the encircling latticework of submerged roots. Here we tied up the horses by their reins to branches and set off, Rafael with his rifle still slung over his shoulder in case of hostile wild life, I with a spare machete in case of further entanglements, and Caroline with her bottle of Scotch in case of less definable emergencies.

'It's not far now,' volunteered Rafael over his shoulder to Caroline in an encouraging tone. 'I can smell the sea already.'

He was right. Soon the mangrove began to thin out; the water through which we were wading (mostly knee deep as Cienfuegos had recorded) was salt; we could hear the rhythmic lap of waves. Despite our compass bearing we did not strike the sea precisely at the Bay of Santa Maria, but when we emerged from the mangroves we could see the bay to our right, to the westward. The beach looked narrow, with trees almost down to the water's edge, and it was difficult to visualize Morgan and his men, aided by his prisoners from Puerto Principe, slaughtering the five hundred head of cattle and salting them on the spot. But when we went over to the beach we found there was indeed a natural causeway of dry land right down to it; if we had hit this in the first place, our approach to the sea would have been immeasurably eased.

We had completed the outward leg of our journey. Rafael was anxious that we should waste no time before tackling the return, since – despite our having set off from a point well to the south of Camaguey – it would take us all our time to get back to his farm that night. We were also encouraged to return to the horses as soon as possible by the fact that our rations were in the saddle-bags on Rafael's horse, and plodding through mangrove swamp had proved hungry work.

I had wondered whether we would have difficulty in finding the small knoll on which we had left the horses tethered. We did not, but the circumstances which made it easy for us were hardly encouraging. While I reckoned we were still some hundred yards away, we heard sounds of panic: there are few more distressing noises in the world than the high-pitched neighing of a terrified horse. It galvanized all of us, and Rafael quickened his pace (which meant that we all did – the thought of being left behind in these surroundings was not appealing).

It was Caroline's horse which was going berserk. Just as we got into view, it broke loose and set off on a series of violent plunges among the mangrove roots. Rafael lurched after it and eventually with difficulty secured it.

'Well, that was lucky,' I said.

'I'm still worried,' said Rafael. 'That horse wouldn't panic without reason. Something must have gone wrong.'

He started to lead the horse back slowly, and it resisted staunchly. Suddenly the horse reared up again, and simultaneously Rafael froze to the spot.

'Stop! Look!' he said, unslinging his rifle with one hand and pointing directly towards the knoll with the other.

I could see nothing. Nor could Caroline. We all three advanced half a dozen paces; then it was Caroline's turn to freeze:

'There – look!'

I stared in the direction of her pointing arm. In front of us appeared the usual gnarled configuration of mangrove roots, interspersed with low mudbanks and tangled foliage. What had they seen? It was like looking for a pattern in one of those books of coloured dots designed to test the colour-blind. Then, suddenly, it all took shape: two well-camouflaged alligators lay almost touching each other on the soft mud slope of our

knoll. One of them – about nine feet long – had its mouth half
open, as if it were a stuffed museum piece in a characteristic
pose.

'No need to shoot them,' said Rafael. 'Now we've seen them,
they can't do us any harm. But there may be others with them
. . . sociable creatures, alligators . . . they like to stay in a
bunch.'

We scanned the other mudbanks nervously. No other shapes
identified themselves. But Rafael decided he wouldn't get
Caroline's horse any closer, so while we held it he advanced,
untethered the others and rejoined us.

Our encounter would not have surprised Morgan. Indeed,
Esquemeling was obsessed about the danger of alligators and
their closely related cousins, caymans. Although he does not
recount any specific encounters with them on the march to
Puerto Principe, he does describe various tussles between
buccaneers and alligators and caymans. On one occasion, for
instance, he recalls:

> a certain person of good reputation and credit told me that
> one day he was by the riverside, washing his tent . . . a
> cayman fastened upon the tent, and with incredible fury
> dragged it under the water. The man, desirous to see if he
> could save his tent, pulled on the contrary side with all his
> strength, having in his mouth a butcher's knife to defend
> himself in case of urgent necessity. The cayman, being angry
> at this opposition, vaulted upon his body, out of the river,
> and drew him with great celerity into the water, endeav-
> ouring with the weight of his bulk to stifle him under the
> banks.

The cayman, it turned out, was no match for the buccaneer's
knife work in the water, and we are told that it 'suddenly
expired'. Even if Esquemeling's companions did not fear immediate attack by the Spaniards, while they were operating on
land they would customarily keep watch at night for fear of
alligators. On the Isle of Pines, to the west of the Bay of Santa

An alligator encountered near the bay of Santa Maria

Maria further along the south coast of Cuba, Esquemeling recounts how an alligator (which he here calls a crocodile) assaulted a buccaneer:

> and fastening upon his leg, cast him upon the ground. Yet he, notwithstanding, being a robust and courageous man, drew forth a knife he had then about him, and with the same, after a dangerous combat, overcame and killed the crocodile. Which having done, he himself, weakened with the loss of blood that ran from his wounds, lay for dead upon the place, or at least beside his senses.

However, he recovered and his companions set out on a mighty alligator hunt in revenge, only being deterred when one of the beasts 'began to mount the ladder of their ship'. Clearly the buccaneer practice of 'having a knife about one' in case of such 'urgent necessity' was a minimal precaution in these parts.

The alligator incident had taken some time. Now it was more than ever necessary to press on if we were even to regain the savannah country before nightfall. We did not relish the idea of a night march in the Che Guevara tradition. Perhaps because the horses were tired, or perhaps because we ourselves were less observant now, the occurrence of plunges into watery pot-holes in the *manigua* seemed more frequent on the return. When eventually we emerged on to harder ground, our faces and necks were streaked with trickles of blood, and our clothes were ripped in all directions: the thorns had taken their toll as well as the pot-holes.

Now our progress was silent. No more did Rafael regale us with stories, and no more did we ply him with bright and lively questions. It was some time before Caroline and I noticed that we were returning by a slightly different route from that which we had taken on the outward journey. It hardly seemed worth the effort of asking why.

The reason, had we enquired, was that our new track led us past an isolated farm called – improbably – Arizona. As we approached, a woman and a number of small boys emerged, the latter running towards us with the enthusiasm that young children in solitary places reserve for unexpected visitors. It was not until we dismounted at the gate of the farm that we realized what bad shape we were in. Caroline and I, after fourteen hours of bracing ourselves against the stresses and strains of misplaced feet (our own and our horses) and mis-shaped saddles, found we could scarcely stand. Like two old age pensioners we hobbled arm in arm through the gate, through the open farm door and on to a wooden bench against the wall. Rafael was busy explaining us, just out of earshot (what explanation could he be volunteering?), and then the farmer's wife appeared with tin mugs of hot bean soup or stew.

Eventually everyone settled on benches round the walls and a general conference ensued. It was concluded that it was too late to complete the ride to Rafael's home farm that night. The best plan would be to sleep at Arizona; beds there were not, but cushions, blankets and the benches provided a good deal better billet than many an airport lounge. Caroline had not forgotten to bring her bottle in from her saddle-bag: now it was passed round and the same tin mugs were filled with generous tots. Rafael again became communicative:

'This is an historic building. It may not have been here when your pirate came through' (all Cubans described Drake and Morgan as pirates) 'but it was certainly here when I went through with Camilo Cienfuegos in 1958. He always said it was the most comfortable night he spent during all his thirty-one days in Camaguey province, and also the most dangerous. Somehow the Batista forces had got wind of the fact that some of Castro's men were in these parts, and a contingent in jeeps turned up before first light in the morning. We only just had time to bundle Camilo upstairs to the loft before the pigs came in with their rifles and bayonets, prodding all around. Eventually they pushed off because their officer said that as there were no horses here, there couldn't be any guerrillas. Never occurred to them that we could *walk* through this sort of country.'

Sleep did not come easily. As I lay shifting position on a hard bench, trying to avoid resting on bruised parts of my anatomy, I experienced grave doubts about what I was up to: not doubts about why I had come, or even about why I had allowed Caroline to expose herself to this hard-sought discomfort; we had voluntarily let ourselves in for whatever might happen to us. My doubts centred on Rafael and, looking back, on Angel, the fisherman who had befriended me among the cays of San Felipe. What right had we, who were shortly to return to all the comforts of diplomatic life in the metropolis, to encourage others whose lives were one permanent chapter of hardships to add to the sum of their discomfort by associating themselves with my selfish and quirky quest? The old adage that the greatest luxury of all is to be able to relish temporary discomfort struck me with a new force. And yet, I thought, if one of the purposes of being in this country at all was to understand the people who lived here, then that purpose was being better fulfilled by lying on a hard bench at 1 a.m. in Arizona than by sitting at a diplomatic dinner party in Havana. And since communication is a two-way process, perhaps – in some broader sense – Rafael and Angel were not wasting their time either

Caroline emerges scratched and exhausted from the *manigua*

by presenting their own hardy facets of the Cuban scene to me. Eventually I fell asleep and dreamed of shouting messages to Rafael down a long hollow mangrove root which was suddenly severed by being bitten in two by a berserk alligator.

In the morning Caroline and I were still so stiff we could hardly walk; but we completed the ride to Rafael's farm and had a small celebration and an affectionate leave-taking. Although the trip had had its hardships and excitements for us, I feared it would not pass into the annals of the memorable for Rafael.

We had one piece of unfinished business in Camaguey. Although not much remained of the original structure of the churches in which Morgan had rounded up the inhabitants of the captured town, I had been told by the Cuban national historian in Havana that there were some local records of Morgan's raid which were still extant but never inspected. With a little local help we traced these down to the former Bishop's Palace, a charming old colonial-style building with stone and wooden cloisters constructed round a central patio. Here an ancient custodian – a layman with a reverence unusual in Cuba for things ecclesiastical – took dusty volumes out of wooden presses. Oh yes, he said, the diocesan records went back a very long time, to Easter 1668, in fact.

'What a coincidence,' I said. 'That's exactly when Captain Morgan raided Puerto Principe.'

'Hardly a coincidence,' came the reply. 'Look at the very first entry in the first volume of our "Record of Baptism of White Children".'

I did. It was written in a faded but clearly legible Spanish hand, and read in translation:

The English enemy entered this town at daybreak on the Thursday of Holy Week the 29th of March 1668 and burnt all the records of previous baptisms, and they left on the 1st of April, on the morning of the Resurrection of Our Lord which thus served to liberate us also from our misfortunes. Francisco Galceran.

There was something poignant about the fact that, after all his rapine and pillage, the only remaining accusation against Henry Morgan here on the site of his monstrous conduct was the charge that he had destroyed the records. The scribes had had the last word.

6

Wickedness at Portobello

The capture of Puerto Principe in early 1668 had been Morgan's first major personal triumph, and the sack of Panama City in 1671 was to be his crowning glory (or crime – depending on one's point of view). But between these campaigns there were two expeditions which, in their own quite different ways, were his most classic achievements: the raids on Portobello in mid-1668 and on the Gulf of Maracaibo in 1669.

However daring and remarkable had been Morgan's venture to the Cuban interior, it had not proved very profitable. Meat and hides were no substitute for bullion. Morgan's French associates were so disappointed that they defected, and his English buccaneers required from their admiral a more lucrative objective for their next sortie.

No destination on the whole Spanish Main conjured up such dreams of avarice as the sleepy little town of Portobello on the Caribbean coast of Panama. This was not a thriving metropolis like Havana, or a mighty seaport like Cartagena; it was a small settlement which only came to life once every couple of years when the Spanish galleons put in to collect the silver which had been brought from the mines of Potosí – up the Peruvian coast to Panama City and across the isthmus by mule – before being shipped back to Spain. It came to life because the galleons not only collected silver: they also brought every sort of consumer commodity which the citizens of Portobello and – more importantly – of Panama City wanted. When the galleons were in harbour, a two-week fair ensued, of which a first-hand account has come down to us from a most unusual source: a book called 'The English-American' which is not only available to us but which was also available to Morgan.

Wickedness at Portobello

Wickedness at Portobello   123

Thomas Gage, the author of this remarkable work, was an Englishman born around 1600 into an old Catholic family. He studied in Jesuit seminars in Spain, was bilingual in Spanish and became a Roman Catholic priest. Indeed, he was accepted by the ever-suspicious Spanish colonial authorities and allowed to travel throughout the length and breadth of their empire, preaching, administering masses and, more sinisterly, taking notes. Ultimately he returned to England and abjured his religion; he encouraged Cromwell to launch his 'Western Design' against the Spanish possessions in the New World and gave evidence during Popery scares against his former coreligionists, many of whom suffered grievously in consequence. He remains something of an enigma: not a very likeable man, but a very astute observer.

Gage had stayed at Portobello for some weeks in 1637, before and during the celebrated fair. (It was here, incidentally, that he recounted having grave doubts for the first time about the doctrine of transubstantiation, as a result of seeing a mouse eat the consecrated Host during the service of Mass – an incident which he recounts in a contentiously pseudo-theological way.) He had complained bitterly about the extortionate cost of lodgings and food during the period of the fair, but – more interestingly for Morgan – he had recorded that the town filled up with silver: not only the storehouses but even the streets and squares were piled with bars unloaded from the mule trains and awaiting shipment to Spain.

Morgan could not, of course, have contemplated an attack during the biennial visit of the galleons: the harbour at that time was crammed with warships and the town with soldiers. But he rightly calculated that a good deal of money stuck to the fingers of the Portobello merchants, and that the town would have a much higher ransom value than Puerto Principe. The main problem was that it boasted no less than three major fortresses. Some of these were known to contain English prisoners, including – it was alleged – Prince Maurice, the brother of Prince Rupert and the cousin of Charles II, who had been lost and assumed captured in these waters some years before. The prospect of releasing prisoners and – the classic pretext – pre-empting an attack on Jamaica was sufficient justification for what looked like being a very profitable raid.

Surprise was imperative. The fortresses had permanent garrisons which, according to report, were lax and unprepared. But however dozy they might be, the sudden appearance of a flotilla of strange ships on the horizon would galvanize them into action. Morgan therefore decided to revert to the mode of travel to which he had been reduced on his return from his Mexican raids three years before: he put his men into twenty-three canoes. With a single escort ship to shadow them, he crept down the coast and anchored off a small island several miles from the entrance to Portobello harbour. The escort ship was spotted, but the canoes were invisible from that distance and so no general alarm was raised.

Morgan and his men paddled inshore under cover of darkness. At that point their luck ran out. The crew of a rowing-boat, which had been sent out from the town the evening before to investigate the unidentified ship, heard the splash of paddles and the chatter of foreign voices – west-country oaths? – over the still waters; they did not wait to enquire further, but turned and sped for home, firing in the air and shouting their warning as their tiny craft hurtled into the sleeping harbour. The citizens of Portobello panicked: a raid by the English buccaneers was what they had always dreaded but never prepared for. Some took to the hills in their nightshirts, others stashed their valuables down wells or under beds, and a few even made their way to one or other of the fortresses to swell the ranks of the garrison.

As was his custom, Morgan landed his men a mile or two from his destination and made his attack overland rather than directly from the sea. This was one of the lessons he had learnt from Mings at Santiago in Cuba. In this case he found it impossible to circumvent the castle of Santiago (there was a certain repetitiousness in Spanish place names) which was situated squarely between his landing-place and the town; but happily the castle's cannon had not been loaded with grapeshot and were in any case so badly handled that Morgan's men passed under their muzzles with impunity. Once inside the town itself, the buccaneers found that not many of the startled citizens attempted to resist their slashing cutlasses as they made their way to the Royal Treasury and hacked the shackles off the ankles and wrists of the English prisoners, among whom – alas – there was no sign of Prince Maurice; those released recalled that 'a great man had been carried thence six months before', so the legend that the Prince was still in Spanish hands persisted. The former captives showed Morgan how best to assault the second castle, San Geronimo. This, together with the whole town, had fallen into their hands by sunrise on that 26th of June, 1668.

Morgan could not relax yet, however. The bypassed castle of Santiago and the third citadel – that of San Felipe de Todo Fierro (St Philip All of Iron) across the bay – still commanded the entrance to the harbour. If he were to carry off the plunder he expected and make a safe and fast getaway, he would have to bring his four frigates and various smaller craft into port, and this meant first silencing the guns of the citadels. Buccaneer sharpshooters were already busily picking off the gunners on the ramparts of Santiago. But this was slow work and Morgan resolved on a quicker and less orthodox expedient: he selected from among his prisoners those who would evoke the greatest public sympathy – elders of the city and priests, young girls and nuns. These he marched to the approaches to the castle of Santiago and then, at pike-point, right up to the gates, using them as a shield for his own demolition squad with their axes and fire-brands. Reluctantly and too late the garrison fired chainshot into the hostages and assailants; but the gates were reached and breached, and soon all that remained to be done was to pile up the bodies of the defendants (among which one live Spaniard survived unnoticed for four days).

The castle of San Felipe held out longer because it was further away and better armed. Its problem was that no one had thought to store any food within its confines: a daily shopping run had been made to the town, and now that this source of

The seventeenth-century fortress overlooking the entrance to
Portobello harbour

supply was cut off the *castellan* was apprehensive about how
long he could survive. Morgan and his men crossed the bay and
began what they expected to be a prolonged assault. (Neither
side knew that plans had been made by refugees from the town
to smuggle food into the castle at night.) The *castellan* lost his
nerve and – on his own initiative – started to parley with the
buccaneers, who used the diversion to launch undetected
attacks from unexpected quarters. It was never safe to assume
that because Morgan was talking he had given up fighting. Soon
the buccaneers were masters of San Felipe too, and the unhappy
castellan, double-crossed by Morgan about the surrender terms
and disgraced in the eyes of his own men, asked his captors to
give him a flask of vitriol to drink. They obligingly complied.

Now at last it was time for the looting to begin. Morgan's men
had not been squeamish at Puerto Principe, but here they
excelled themselves in devising ways to induce the citizens to
divulge the hiding-places of their treasures. Mr Peter Earle,

who has researched the incidents from both the Spanish and the English sides, quotes* grisly details of prisoners who were (according to one Spanish narrator) 'burnt in parts that for decency he will not refer to' and of a woman 'set bare upon a baking stove and roasted'. It seems that some of the more sluttish women of Portobello not only encouraged the amorous advances of the buccaneers but gave information about the wealthier of the respectable matrons, which led to the latter being selected for the baking stoves. But although much more jewellery and plate came to light than at Puerto Principe, Morgan concluded that the way to consolidate his profits was to demand a ransom for the town as a whole: it would be burnt, the castles blown up, the guns thrown into the sea and the citizens carried off as slaves unless the Spanish governor of Panama City (on the other side of the peninsula) came forward with a ransom of 350,000 pesos.

The governor had no intention of negotiating payments to corsairs. He had already started to march an army across the peninsula and now sent a firm message back. Morgan, having ambushed the approaching army, wrote a further insolent demand, dated from 'Portobello, City of the King of England', despite the fact that Charles II knew nothing about the raid and his kingdom was nominally at peace with Spain. Notwithstanding the bravado, in reality both sides were getting apprehensive: the Spanish troops were suffering from everything from fever to foot-rot, and Morgan's men were beginning to be smitten with the same ailments. As so often, it was disease rather than battle casualties that brought hostilities to a close.

At length a more reasonable ransom figure was agreed. 100,000 pesos' worth of bars of silver, silver plate, and gold and silver coin were dispatched in two mule-trains from Panama City to Portobello. When eventually the buccaneers sailed out of Portobello harbour exactly a month after they had arrived they were carrying a total of some 250,000 pesos' worth of loot. This was a far larger haul than any previous venture had produced. Converting such sums into modern currency is

* *The Sack of Panama* (London, 1981)

misleading, but Mr Dudley Pope has calculated★ that it amounted to the value of ten per cent of the total exports from all the West Indian plantations for a whole year, and about sixty per cent of the value of a year's exports from London to all the plantations. Even after the King's and the Duke of York's shares had been deducted, the ordinary buccaneer's share amounted to the equivalent of several years' wages for a common sailor or soldier. It was little wonder that the revels in Port Royal after their return were still remembered seventy years later – after the destruction of the city – when Charles Leslie was writing his history of Jamaica. It was Port Royal's finest hour. Portobello on the other hand was never quite the same again.

It was certainly not the same when I jolted in my little hired car up the twenty miles of rough track – a diversion from the main road across the isthmus of Panama – to the now almost deserted village of Portobello. The road ran parallel to the coast, through banana groves and palm trees; as one house or farmstead after another was left behind, the track became ever rougher and one wondered whether it might not give up the struggle to survive before it reached Portobello. Then, quite suddenly, I rounded yet another corner and saw ahead of me one of the most beautiful bays on the whole coast of Central America. No wonder it had been called the beautiful port by its early Spanish discoverers! The sanctimonious Gage and the censorious Esquemeling had given no hint of the charm of the place, of the bright blue fringe of water forming a shapely bay between green wooded banks. I wished that this had been one of those stages on my pilgrimage around Morgan's haunts on which Caroline had been able to join me (had I known how it was going to work out, I would perhaps have thought otherwise).

Even when it was many months away from the biennial fair, Portobello in the seventeenth century can hardly have been as dormant as in the twentieth. I parked the car where the road finally expired in the village centre. There were two or three rows of houses (the South American Handbook claims that

★ *Harry Morgan's Way* (London, 1977)

1,980 people live here, but I couldn't think where they all found to sleep) and a parish church which was called the cathedral. Even from here I could see the crenellated battlements along the waterfront.

In fact, two of the main fortresses which Morgan had captured – Santiago and San Geronimo – appeared to be in a state of excellent repair. The Spaniards had, as usual, shut and locked the stable door after the horse had bolted: there were wide gun terraces, still with rows of cannon; pepper-pot lookout towers; deep fosses with steep, stone-lined sides; walls and gatehouses. I clambered over them, measuring, photographing and trying to visualize the scene as the defenders of these battlements eventually steeled themselves to fire into the screen of nuns and children which Morgan was alleged to have driven up to the gates in front of his own men.

In the cathedral a small child took me to see the great relic of the place: the Black Christ. This carved wooden statue was intended as a gift from Spain to the Viceroy of Peru, but the ship in which it was making its crossing had been sunk at the approaches to Portobello (no one could tell me exactly when this had happened, or whether the buccaneers had helped it on its way to the bottom) and the carving had lain for many years on the seabed, thus acquiring – by popular report – its black patina. It looked to me suspiciously as if it had always been black; could the Spaniards have decided that their mission work in the distant empire would be assisted by this representation of a non-European deity?

Having completed my tour of inspection, I wandered along the western bank of the bay towards a promontory with shady trees and green grass – a perfect picnic place for eating the sandwiches which I had brought. Across the bay I could see a luxury yacht moored well out from the shore. There seemed to be some activity on board; a dinghy was alongside. I raised the binoculars which I always carry on such trips to get a better look. I was so intent on the distant scene that I did not hear the quiet approach of suède shoes across the grass.

'You from the Agency?'

I nearly jumped out of my skin. A tall, clean-shaven American was standing beside me looking down at my binoculars and my half-eaten sandwiches. He wore a white shirt, black knitted tie and button-down collar, and smelt faintly of after-shave.

'You from the Agency?' he repeated.

'Agency?' I said, scrambling to my feet in order to feel less dominated by this intruder on my solitary picnic. 'What agency? I'm not from any agency. Who are you? What do you want?' Asking questions made me feel less vulnerable.

'Just a coincidental interest in *La Belle Epoque*?' He pronounced it to rhyme with soliloquy.

'If you're talking about that yacht,' I said, 'it isn't *La Belle Epoque* anyway: it's the *Tamarisk*. And why shouldn't I be looking at it? Very pretty yacht.' I was still feeling encroached upon and defensive.

'No offence meant. Guess we're both right. Take another look at the stern where the name's painted. See anything odd about it?' He produced his own binoculars and trained them on the yacht.

I followed his line of gaze but could see nothing remarkable. The man on board was still fiddling around with the dinghy in the way yachtsmen do so endlessly. Everything else looked shipshape to me.

'Look at the name,' my companion went on. 'See anything funny about the paintwork? Name's in black, isn't it? And the hull's white. Black lettering stands out on a white hull with no bother, right? So why do you think there's a panel of lighter white paint round the name? I'll tell you why: it's because another name's been painted out, that's why. And the panel's longer than the new name, right? That's because the old name was a longer name than the new one, right? Like the name *La Belle Epoque* is longer than *Tamarisk*, right?'

'Right,' I said. 'But new owners often change the names of their yachts. Some people think it's unlucky, but it's not a crime. Or are you suggesting that the yacht might have been stolen?'

'Worse. Much worse. Perhaps it's time I introduced myself,'

he said. 'Omar S. Reinburger – Drug Enforcement Administration – glad to meet you. Mind if I sit down and talk? I've got a problem . . . a right big problem . . . and it sure would help to talk to somebody who looks like he isn't a dago or a goddam pusher.'

Mr Reinburger (which was not his name, but it will serve) sat himself down beside me on the grass overlooking the ruins of the fortress of Santiago and told me a story as violent and melodramatic as any which might have been connected with that ancient blood-soaked edifice.

The hinterland of Colombia, despite strenuous efforts by its government, was still – he explained – one of the most productive areas in the world for the growing of cocaine and marijuana. The most lucrative market for these drugs was the United States, and the easiest places at which to land consignments of them were on the jungle-clad coastline of Florida or on impromptu airstrips cleared in the Everglades swamps. The profits for those who converted the cheaply produced crop into a desperately sought-after black-market commodity were such as to cause greed and violence on an international scale. The only problem was transportation. Much of the cocaine and marijuana was flown from Colombia to Florida in light private aircraft, refuelling during the long Caribbean flight at unfrequented landing-strips in remote islands of the Turks and Caicos or other groups. But much more went by sea, avoiding the frequented holiday islands of the Caribbean in favour of routes where unwanted attentions were unlikely. The risks of the sea route became greatest as the seaboard of the United States was approached: coastguard vessels and spotter planes might pick up notorious or even suspicious craft. For an untroubled landing a 'clean' yacht was required: one which had never been used on a drugs run before and which never would be again. There was an almost indefinite supply of such yachts from the pleasure harbours of the West Indies. It was no good stealing these yachts from their moorings at English Harbour in Antigua or at Bridgetown in Barbados; their loss would be reported immediately and a description of the yacht circulated to coastguards throughout the Caribbean. To be useful to the drug-runners the yachts had to be seized at sea, far from prying gaze. Smuggling begot piracy.

It was a particularly brutal form of piracy which Mr Reinburger outlined to me. The drug-runners who set sail from the north coast of Colombia – often in pairs of speedboats seeking their prey – did not give quarter to their victims; not for them the seventeenth-century civilities of putting captured crews ashore or ransoming them; these smugglers wanted no witnesses, and many a young couple on a honeymoon cruise, or elderly playboy with his guests, had been brutally gunned down and tossed to the sharks for the sake of their 'clean' yacht. In the previous three years alone, Mr Reinburger told me, over a thousand people had been murdered in these waters; often it was assumed at first that they had been lost at sea due to bad weather or bad seamanship; only much later might their abandoned yacht, its name changed, be found in some Florida creek, or discovered scuttled off some deserted shore, and the grim truth would be recognized. The ranks of the big-time smugglers were swelled by more casual sea-wolves; prudent yachtsmen carried firearms in these waters and ran for harbour at the appearance of strange vessels.

'Now the *Belle Epoque* went missing about two months ago,' Mr Reinburger went on. 'The crew were a forty-year-old Wall Street broker, his wife and two teenage kids . . . sailed from Port of Spain, Trinidad . . . bound for a cruise of the Windward Islands . . . never seen again . . . no reported storms . . . experienced sailors . . . all very odd.'

'But what makes you think the *Tamarisk* might be her?' I was quite unconvinced.

'Tip-off. The D.E.A. have a few chaps down this coast keeping their eyes open for missing yachts of US registration. One of them called up the Embassy. They got on to me and I drove down. See this photo? That's the *Belle Epoque*. Same Bermuda rig, same line, same everything as the boat in front of you – except the name. And except the crew. *Tamarisk* has three men aboard, all in their thirties I'd guess, look like Latinos.

There's that chap you see fiddling around with the dinghy and two more below now.'

'But why should they be here? Portobello's hardly on a line from Trinidad to Florida.'

'They probably took her down to the Colombian coast first, loaded her up with hash, and are now sneaking up the peninsula to the north. These chaps like to give Cuba a wide berth . . . don't blame them . . . too many patrol boats round that coast . . . and friend Fidel doesn't go much on dope pushers . . . get a stiffer sentence there than they would in the States.'

The whole thing seemed like a bad dream. Here I was sitting picnicking on a delightful headland, overlooking one of the most enchanting bays in the Carribean, watching a beautiful yacht ride at her moorings, when suddenly a stranger had intruded on my idyll and persuaded me that I was witnessing a modern drama of crime and violence.

'How will you know if you're right?' I asked. 'And what can you do about it?'

'Just sit around and you'll see. Keep your eye on the entrance to the bay. We've alerted the local coastguards. Shouldn't be long to wait now.' Mr Reinburger looked at a digital watch and then resumed his study of the *Tamarisk* through his giant binoculars.

'Say! Look at that, now! More patches of fresh paintwork round the wheelhouse.' He appeared to be getting excited. 'Sure sign of patching up after a gunfight . . . holes filled in and painted over . . . seen it often before . . .'

'It looks to me,' I said, 'as if the chap on deck is about to go ashore in his dinghy.'

Even as I spoke, the dinghy cast off and, with one man aboard, headed down the bay towards the harbour, its noisy outboard motor audible from where we sat.

Mr Reinburger was on his feet in a bound. 'I'd better go see what he's up to. Maybe he's got a rendezvous.' He disappeared as suddenly as he had arrived.

At that moment a trim, naval-looking cutter rounded the wooded point at the entrance to the bay, a red, blue and white

Another aspect of the entrance to Portobello harbour where the
Tamarisk rode at anchor

Panamanian flag fluttering from her stern. The high bows looked
as if made for speed and the mounted machine-gun on the stern
as if meant for business.

At the same time as I saw the cutter, the man in the dinghy
also saw her. He put his hand down on the rudder, turned his
little craft round 180 degrees and made straight back to the
yacht. By the time he reached it, the other two crew members
were already on deck and the powerful engine had been started
(there was no attempt to set the sails). The man from the dinghy
jumped aboard, abandoning his dinghy without attempting to
secure it to the yacht, which motored straight across the bay to
the side on which I was sitting and turned towards the sea while
at the same time hugging the near shoreline.

By this manoeuvre the cutter, now in the centre of the bay,
was prevented from approaching the yacht too closely because
of the risk of running aground on account of its deeper draught.

I watched the yacht proceed up the western side of the bay, keeping close in, while the naval craft shadowed it from further out in deep water. Both vessels rounded the point of the bay and were lost to sight – but not to hearing.

First I heard a tannoy, presumably from the cutter; it was too far off to pick out the words, but I could catch from their tone that orders were being given, first in Spanish and then in English. This was repeated several times, getting fainter as the vessels got further away.

Then followed – quite unmistakably – a burst of small arms fire, and something hit with a thud one of the higher branches of the tree under which I was sitting.

Now finally any hope was destroyed of my picnic remaining a peaceful meditation on the scene of Morgan's former conquests: the violence of the twentieth century had intruded on the ghosts of the seventeenth. I packed up and returned to my hired car, and turning my back on Portobello, began driving back down the rough road towards the Canal.

I had not gone half a mile when an agitated figure jumped out of a large car parked beside the track. It was Mr Reinburger. He waved me to stop.

'Did you see what happened?'

'No,' I said.

'They tried to get away in the yacht. But the coastguard cutter hailed them and told them to haul to. They didn't. So the cutter fired across their bows. Then the three men abandoned *Tamarisk* and swam ashore – just up there, where the trees go down to the water. Now we've lost them. They can't get far, but they'll be armed, so don't give a lift to any strangers!'

Mr Reinburger resumed scanning the woods. As he raised his powerful binoculars I now noticed an ominous bulge under his left armpit: it was not only the crew of *Tamarisk* who might be armed.

'Tell me one thing,' I said. 'How did you know I wasn't one of the smugglers myself, waiting for a rendezvous with the *Tamarisk*?'

'Good question. You had me worried when I first saw you

drive into Portobello and start sniffing around the shore. See this? That's a car radio transmitter, right? I just did a quick check up on your registration number with my chief in Panama City. He came back ten minutes later and said yours was a vehicle hired yesterday by a gringo with an introduction from the British Embassy. That's why I guessed you were on the same job as me – criminal investigation.'

'In a sense I am,' I said. 'The difference is that the crime that brings me here happened three hundred years ago.'

Mr Reinburger was still looking puzzled as I watched him recede into the distance in my rear mirror.

It is a recurring theme of biographies of Sir Henry Morgan that he was a better soldier than sailor; his most imaginative exploits were almost always on land – his surprise marches on Villa-hermosa and Puerto Principe, and his unconventional overland assaults on more than a dozen fortresses and towns. But one encounter alone entitles him to consideration as a naval commander of imagination: his escape from the lagoon of Maracaibo in 1669.

How he came to be trapped in the lagoon in the first place is a less glorious story. It began with the loss of the best flagship he ever had – the thirty-four-gun frigate *Oxford* which had been sent by the Navy Board (served by Samuel Pepys) in London to strengthen the seaborne defences of Jamaica. As so often, Governor Modyford had decided that the best method of defence was attack: he had handed over the *Oxford* to the buccaneer captain, who had promptly captured another four-teen-gun ship. Morgan now felt that he had a regular naval force for once, and he and his captains decided – in their own distinctive and democratic manner – that a worthy target should be attacked: no less a place than Cartagena itself, the main fortress-port of the whole Spanish Main. It was probably an overaudacious target even for a well-fitted-out frigate and supporting vessels (and indeed Morgan was later to shy away from Cartagena when he had a far larger force at his command), but for the moment no objective seemed too ambitious.

It was while celebrating this bold decision that disaster overtook them. Morgan and his captains were seated below decks in the *Oxford*, drinking and singing (according to Esquemeling), while a number of prisoners were locked up in the hold, when by some freak or accident, carelessness or sabotage the powder magazine blew up. The frigate was blasted in an instant to matchwood; some two hundred men were also blown to smithereens or drowned as a result of the explosion and shock. Only six men and four boys from the entire crew survived.

Miraculously, among the survivors was Henry Morgan. By a quirk of the blast, those captains who had sat on his side of the heavy oak wardroom table were tossed into the sea alive, while those opposite were picked up from the sea in pieces.

When the news of the loss of the *Oxford* reached the Spanish inhabitants of Cartagena, they realized that they were reprieved and attributed their deliverance to the patron saint of the city – *Nuestra Señora de la Popa* – who 'was abroad the night the *Oxford* man-of-war was blown up . . . and came home all wet' (according to the accounts which later reached William Dampier, the buccaneer and explorer). There may have been other Spaniards who felt that the saint might have made a more thorough job of it by ensuring that Morgan had not survived the blast.

The sinking of the *Oxford* was indeed a deliverance for Cartagena. Having lost his flagship and two hundred of his men, Morgan was obliged to look for a softer target. The lagoon of Maracaibo, leading out of the Gulf of Venezuela, had a number of prosperous little towns on its shores and had not been raided by the Jamaican privateers before, nor indeed by anyone for a year or two, since the French pirate known as L'Ollonais had made a profitable excursion there. It seemed an attractive – if more modest – substitute for Cartagena.

Even this destination proved almost beyond the grasp of Morgan's much reduced force. When his ships approached the narrow straits leading from the gulf into the lagoon (see map) they discovered that the Spaniards had built a new fort commanding the bottleneck. Shots rang out from its cannon across their bows. Morgan resolved to land a party and make a night attack; he expected – at the very least – a stiff fight.

But as at Portobello, the Spanish physical defences were better than their garrisons. Manpower shortages (there were always many Spaniards sick on the Main) and inefficiency had left a total of one officer and eight soldiers to man the new fort. When Morgan's men scaled the walls and broke in, they could not find a single defender; Esquemeling recounts that they sensed a trap and instituted a rapid search which revealed – with only minutes to spare – a lighted fuse leading to the powder magazine. For the second time inside a few weeks Morgan appeared to be leading a charmed life.

Exhilarated by his good fortune, Morgan made one of his rare strategic errors – one which was nearly to cost him and his men their lives. He decided not to garrison the fort with his own men, thus protecting their retreat, but merely to make a hurried and inadequate job of dismantling its defences. He then inched his little fleet cautiously across the bar and through the sandbanks into the enclosed lagoon of Maracaibo, an inland sea some ninety miles long and sixty miles broad.

The buccaneers at once set about their usual greedy and brutal practices. First Maracaibo itself, then the village of Gibraltar and other smaller settlements round the lagoon were sacked and looted. Escaping citizens were rounded up and tortured to disgorge their valuables. The usual haul of jewellery, pieces of eight, church plate and other movables (including ransomable hostages) was loaded on to the ships. Then suddenly the trap snapped shut.

The Spaniards had long had a squadron of warships to protect their possessions in the New World; grandly named the *Armada de Barlovento*, the squadron – often no more than a flotilla – had been alternately reinforced and reduced in strength over the years, according to the state of alarm or of financial stringency that prevailed at any particular moment. In 1668 the two most powerful ships in the squadron had been recalled to Europe, leaving the Spanish admiral – Don Alonzo de Campos – with only three vessels in his Armada. But these alone were more than able to outgun everything the buccaneers had in the water. The Spanish flagship – the *Magdalena* – was a galleon; the *San Luis* was a frigate, and the *Nuestra Señora de la Soledad* was a converted merchant ship. Even this last was superior to anything which Morgan, deprived of his flagship, could produce.

Normally, trying to find the Jamaican buccaneers in the Caribbean was like looking for lightning before it struck. But since the notorious destruction of the *Oxford*, the buccaneers had left a careless trail behind them. Don Alonzo followed up the rumours by sailing his squadron into the gulf of Venezuela; there he heard more definite news that the buccaneers had crossed the bar into the Lagoon of Maracaibo. Better still, he soon discovered for himself that they had left the new fort at the entrance to the lagoon almost intact and ungarrisoned. Overland escape routes from Maracaibo were impossible: forests, mountains and swamps hemmed the buccaneers in, and even if they reached the desolate Caribbean shore, no boats would be there to take them off. Don Alonzo had Morgan effectually bottled up in the lagoon, with no line of retreat except through a superior fleet and past commanding shore batteries. The day of reckoning had come.

It did not take long for Morgan to appreciate his predicament. He told his men of the surrender terms which Don Alonzo offered them, but the recollection of the condition of their shipmates freed from the dungeons of Portobello did not encourage acceptance. Once again Morgan sent back a truculent reply, this time 'dated from His Majesty of England's citty of Marracaia'.

It was easier to be defiant than to devise an escape plan. However, the word soon got back to Don Alonzo that Morgan was mounting guns and carrying out 'improvements' on a large Cuban merchant ship which he had captured in the lagoon. Clearly he was set for a naval battle.

On 27 April 1669, Morgan sailed his little fleet, his

A contemporary impression of Morgan's rout of the Spanish fleet at Maracaibo and his escape past the fort at the entrance to the lagoon

admiral's flag proudly fluttering from the topmast of his Cuban 'prize', towards the *Armada de Barlovento*, which had by then crossed the bar and was lined up across the exit from the lagoon. The Cuban ship headed straight for the *Magdalena*, the Spanish flagship. It appeared that the buccaneers were planning to board and engage in hand-to-hand contest. The Spaniards were undismayed at the prospect: they were well manned, well disciplined, well armed and had inflicted heavy punishment on Morgan's ship before the latter crashed into them. Indeed, the Spanish reaction to finding *Magdalena* grappled to the Cuban ship was not to attempt to cut themselves clear but to land their own boarding party on the attacking ship. No sooner had the Spaniards dropped from their yardarms on to the deck of Morgan's new flagship than two remarkable things happened simultaneously: the buccaneer ship was found to be unmanned and it burst into fierce flames.

The Spaniards had been deceived. The new 'guns' on their Cuban prize were dummies; the sailors' bonnets along the taffrail turned out to be on posts and not on sailors; the crew had been a skeleton one which had abandoned ship from the stern immediately they had cast their grappling irons on to the *Magdalena*, and Morgan's whole new 'flagship' had been converted into a fire-ship filled with tar and other highly inflammable material to be ignited by the retreating crew. It had been inconceivable to Don Alonzo that his opponents should sacrifice their biggest and best ship in this way. Now he found he could not shake the *Magdalena* clear of her burning neighbour; flames rapidly spread from rigging to rigging and from deck to deck; explosions in the Cuban ship hastened the process of contamination. Soon *Magdalena*'s crew too had taken to the longboats or jumped for safety.

The remaining ships of the *Armada de Barlovento* made for the protection of the new fort in the narrows. The buccaneers would not dare to pursue them under the guns of their shore batteries. One made it to safety: the *San Luis* beached herself near the fort and while most of her crew repaired to its shelter with their weapons, a few stayed behind to set fire to her lest – after all – she should fall into buccaneer hands. The other did not: the *Nuestra Señora de la Soledad*'s mooring fouled and by the time she had cut herself clear she could not be prevented from drifting to shore out of range of the fort's guns, where she was an easy prey to buccaneer boarding parties, and was quickly captured. All three ships of the *Armada de Barlovento* were now sunk, destroyed or captured.

But Morgan was not yet out of his predicament. Although he had defeated the squadron which was opposing his exit from the lagoon, there still remained the Spanish fort covering the narrows. The guns which Morgan had so inadequately spiked were already repaired, and others had been added to them. These shore batteries alone were sufficient to sink every one of his little ships as they attempted to gain the open waters of the gulf of Venezuela. Nor would the fort any longer be easy to capture by a land attack. It was now fully and effectively garrisoned by men from the Armada, whose commander – Don Alonzo – saw the prospect of containing Morgan in the lagoon until more ships arrived as the only hope of retrieving his shattered reputation.

Nevertheless, Morgan appeared to be intent on making an overland attack by night. This was what he had done before, and it was what the buccaneers were best at. All through a long hot day Morgan sent canoes loaded with men to the shore at a point near to, but out of range of, the fort; the Spaniards saw the canoes return empty to the ships. They moved the cannons round to the landward side, loaded them with grapeshot rather than ball, and prepared to repel a determined night assault.

Meanwhile, Morgan waited until dark and then loosed his little ships from their moorings and allowed them to drift down on the tide towards the mouth of the lagoon and the menacing fort. The Spanish lookouts were now no longer alert. They were confident that Morgan would not sail with all his men ashore. What they did not know was that the men whom they had seen going ashore in the canoes had not, in fact, been left on the shore but had returned to the ships lying flat on the bottoms of the canoes. The whole buccaneer force was embarked, and as they slipped past the fort to the open sea, Morgan had achieved an escape with his entire personnel, with his new prize flagship – the *Soledad* – and with further booty (including silver salvaged from the burnt-out *Magdalena*) of well over a hundred thousand pieces of eight. Morgan had shown that on water as well as on land he could be a crafty and formidable opponent.

This was one campaign I could not retrace. The town of Maracaibo is now a vast oil-rich city of three-quarters of a million inhabitants; the lagoon is a forest of oil rigs; the surroundings are built up and changed beyond all recognition. One thing only has not changed: the geography. The entrance to the inland sea is still as narrow; the gulf and the lagoon still form the twin halves of a natural egg-timer, and ships trickle through the straits like coloured sand falling from one half to the other. At least, this is how it looked to me as I flew over the five-mile-long General Rafael Urdaneta bridge which now joins the two shores and the string of islands and sandbanks in between. If there is still a fort on one bank, I could not see it. Perhaps someone more successful than the first Spanish garrison and more thorough than Morgan had eventually blown it up properly?

7

Crossing the Isthmus with Morgan

The most spectacular and best-remembered of all Morgan's raids was that on Panama City: boldest in concept, most lucrative in booty, and furthest-reaching in its political consequences, it was the apogee of his meteoric career. Yet, like so many of his exploits, it was executed for a variety of muddled and misrepresented reasons.

Lord Arlington, Charles II's Secretary of State, was working hard for the conclusion of a peace treaty with Spain. He was confident that Sir William Godolphin would shortly be able to negotiate satisfactory terms in Madrid. The Maracaibo affair had been a setback to his plans and in the summer of 1669 he was writing to Governor Modyford in Jamaica that he should 'oblige the privateers to forbear all hostilities at land . . . till we have a firm answer from Spain.'

Whatever his doubts about the likely effects on the security of Jamaica of ceasing prophylactic attacks on the Spanish Main, Modyford had no alternative but to heed these instructions (which Arlington had taken care to present as 'His Majesty's pleasure') and order Morgan and his fleet of privateers to stay away from the Spanish coasts. Only one thing could induce Modyford to change these orders: direct and irrefutable evidence that the Spanish government were planning an imminent assault on Jamaica.

It was Morgan's old friend Captain John Morris who produced the first evidence of Spanish duplicity. He had been combing the cays off the southern coast of Cuba for prizes and had captured a Spanish man-of-war among whose papers were recently signed commissions to attack English ships. This was certainly relevant, but attacking shipping was not the same thing as invading Jamaica: Morris's evidence on its own would never convince Arlington of the need to reopen hostilities. It was another of Morgan's captains – Edward Collier – who produced the really decisive contribution. He had captured, in the course of a foraging expedition, a Spanish privateer called the *Galliardena* whose master made and signed a statement to the effect that in both Cartagena and Panama troops were being armed, trained and prepared for an assault on Jamaica itself. These reports were sent back by Morgan to Modyford at Port Royal, and by him to Lord Arlington in London.

Taken together, the reports seemed sufficient to Sir Thomas Modyford to justify him in commissioning Morgan and his fellow-privateers to undertake a further raid on the Main in order to upset the Spanish preparations. It was out of the question to await an explicit authorization from the Secretary of State before taking such action, firstly because Arlington had already demonstrated a disinclination to reply to Modyford's dispatches, and secondly because an exchange of correspondence never took less than five months and frequently much longer. Events could not wait that long if Jamaica were not to be a Spanish colony once more by the time that Arlington's revised instructions came to hand.

Morgan assembled a fleet at Tortuga in the autumn of 1670. It was a larger fleet than he had ever commanded before, amounting to some thirty-six ships. More significantly still, he had a larger 'army' than he had ever had before, amounting to 1800 men under his command. Many of the men, and eight of the ships, were French – an internationalizing of the expedition which was to bring its own problems.

As always, the first questions for settlement were the terms of service and the division of the spoils, whatever these should be. Such matters too were to create later problems. But at the outset it was amicable enough: five hundred pieces of eight was agreed to be the compensation for the loss of a right leg, six hundred for a right hand . . . and so on. The rates were up on the normal figures because the expectations from such a powerful force

were also up. There was also a new provision to award con-
spicuous gallantry:

> Unto him that in any battle should signalize himself, either
> by entering the first any castle, or taking the Spanish colours
> and setting up the English, they constituted 50 pieces of eight
> for a reward.

More controversial was the percentage of the 'purchase' to be
allocated to the captains and to the admiral himself, who was to
receive one per cent of the whole.

Formalities behind them, the captains next debated the
target for their expedition. Santiago had been proposed by
Modyford but evoked little enthusiasm. There were four other
cities in Spanish America in the second half of the seventeenth
century which were pre-eminent: Veracruz, the port on the
Mexican coast where the gold from the interior was collected for
shipment by the annual *flota*; Panama, the collecting-point on
the coast of the Southern (i.e. Pacific) Ocean for the silver
mined at Potosí and elsewhere in greater Peru; Cartagena, the
mighty fortress on the southern shore of the Caribbean where
many of the galleons assembled; and Havana, the capital of the
rich colony of Cuba and the port where both galleons and *flota*
met together before facing the Atlantic crossing. Surely, it was
argued, such a powerful fleet and army as that now assembled
under Morgan should aim at one of these major prizes? A
successful attack on any one of them would shake the whole
foundation of the Spanish empire in the New World.

Cartagena and Havana (which does not appear to have been
considered as carefully as the others) were both accessible from
the Caribbean, but – just because of this – both had massive
fortifications. Former prisoners reported with awe the height of
the walls, the number and weight of the cannon and the size of
the garrisons. Before the attack on Puerto Principe, it had been
said by some of the buccaneers that 1500 men would be
necessary to attack Havana – their preferred target – with any
chance of success; now that more than this number were

assembled, Havana still seemed out of reach. Veracruz, though further away, was also on the eastern coastline and therefore well prepared to resist maritime attack; and besides, the bullion from the interior of Mexico was not stored there long.

However, the remaining city was both a richer prize and a softer target than any of the others. Richer, because Panama was not only a transit station for bullion, but a residential metropolis of long standing; softer, because at this date no buccaneers were sailing the waters of the Pacific and the burghers of Panama City reckoned that they had a natural protection against attack from the Caribbean in the form of nearly fifty miles of 'impenetrable' jungle and swamp across the isthmus.

The argument that decided the choice of target had a flaw – a flaw which cost Morgan his liberty and nearly cost him his life a year or two later. If the purpose of the expedition were to pre-empt a Spanish attack on Jamaica, Panama was a curious destination to choose. While it was true that the governor of Panama was among those who had been reported as raising recruits to invade Jamaica, this was the only one of the four major cities of the Spanish empire from which such an attack could not – for geographical reasons – be launched. The selection of Panama betrayed the whole venture for what it essentially was: a marauding raid to collect loot. (Comparisons with Drake's raid on Cadiz nearly a century before emphasize the difference in concept and execution: Drake's attack un-doubtedly unsettled and postponed the plans for the Spanish Armada; little profit was generated for the raiders and not a single Spanish civilian was killed.)

But Panama it was to be. And no one was more conscious than Morgan of the limitations of his knowledge about the approaches to the city and the routes across the isthmus. What he did know was that basically there were two routes: the jungle track from Portobello via Venta da Cruz to Panama, and the Chagres river route from Chagres village on the Caribbean coast to Venta da Cruz and then on by the same jungle track to Panama. The disadvantage of the former route – which was the one taken by the mule convoys of plate, once so notably ambushed by Drake – was that it involved attacking Portobello again. This settlement had been refortified since Morgan's earlier assault, and – a more serious snag – the population of Portobello could be relied upon to warn Panama of the impending attack: no sooner would buccaneer sails be seen off the creek at Portobello than messengers would set off down the jungle tracks across the isthmus to inform the governor of what was afoot. Chagres too had its drawbacks: the chief of these was the heavily fortified castle of San Lorenzo on a natural commanding position at the mouth of the Chagres river. Another snag which does not appear to have occurred to Morgan and his associates was that it was extremely unlikely, even if San Lorenzo could be overwhelmed, that this could be done so rapidly that no survivors would escape to carry the tidings to Panama City. Whatever way the buccaneers approached, they were likely to have a stiff preliminary fight and to lose the element of surprise. Nevertheless, the Chagres river was judged the better route.

They were also certain to need guides to lead them up the twisting, overhung waters of the Chagres and through the jungle paths beyond Venta da Cruz. The obvious place to acquire – in effect, to capture – such guides was the island of St Catherine (or Old Providence, as it was more popularly known) for, according to Esquemeling,

> in the garrison of that island are commonly employed many *banditti* and outlaws belonging to Panama and the neighbouring places, who are very expert in the knowledge of all that country.

Morgan, who had transferred his fleet from Tortuga to Cape Tiburon at the western end of Hispaniola, consequently set sail for Old Providence on 16 December 1670. His evacuation of Tortuga and swift departure from Cape Tiburon were perhaps prompted by a premonition – or, more likely, by a suspicion based on rumour – that if he loitered too long he might receive orders to desist from his expedition. Modyford was clearly nervous about authorizing fresh provocations against Spain, but not nearly as nervous as he would have been had he known the turn events were taking in Europe.

The capture of Old Providence was a singularly bizarre incident. There were two islands in the group and Morgan landed with a thousand men on the larger of them, only to find that the island had already been evacuated by the Spanish garrison, who had concentrated themselves on the smaller and heavily defended adjoining island. Morale among the buccaneers deteriorated alarmingly: they had landed without food or warm clothing and torrential tropical rain quickly reduced them to grumbling and talk of return to the boats. Esquemeling – ever given to exaggeration – recorded that they

> were reduced to great affliction and danger of their lives through the hardness of the weather, their own nakedness, and the great hunger they sustained.

Morgan resorted to a bold bluff to put spirit into his own men and to unnerve his opponents: he sent an ultimatum to the garrison commander demanding his immediate surrender on pain of 'being put to the sword, without quarter to any'.

The Spanish commander, though outnumbered, had no reason to listen to such bluster. He had no less than nine fortresses on his tiny island, all of them equipped with an adequate number of well-sited cannon. The main castle was 'commodiously seated on a mountain', and had stone walls and a moat around it. He had fresh water and plentiful provisions. But Morgan's reputation was fearsome. Threats of giving no quarter had all too realistic a ring. The commander spent two hours contemplating and debating the ultimatum and then came up with a most singular response.

He would surrender, but before he did so Morgan must take part in a charade designed to protect the Spanish commander's reputation. The request was that Morgan should make a feint night attack by land on the fort of St Jerome, while at the same time his ships feigned an attack on the fort of St Teresa; Morgan should also put ashore a landing-party to take the shore batteries at St Matthew and then – in Esquemeling's words –

those troops which were newly landed should by this means intercept the Governor by the way, as he endeavoured to pass to St Jerome's fort, and then take him prisoner, using the formality, as if they forced him to deliver the said castle; and that he should lead the English into it, under the fraud of being his own troops; that on one side and the other there should be continual firing at one another, but without bullets, or at least into the air, so that no side might receive any harm by this device.

It suited Morgan well enough to play along with this elaborate subterfuge: 'the propositions – every one – were granted', we are told; but a solemn warning was added against duplicity on the part of the Spaniards, which would result in their being treated 'with all rigours imaginable'. Morgan also warned the governor to keep a tight grip on his men, as any random stragglers were likely to get shot: the buccaneers were a trigger-happy force and unlikely to wait for explanations if the scenario went awry.

It did not. Everything went according to plan: 'the island being taken by this unusual stratagem, and all things put in due order'. This last phrase of Esquemeling's was a euphemism for pillaging the castle and poultry yards and reprovisioning the ships. Now Morgan turned his attention to the original purpose of his coming to Old Providence: the finding of guides 'to show him the securest ways and passages to Panama'. Three *banditti* 'who pretended to be very expert in all the avenues of those parts' offered their services. Morgan recruited them, offering them a share of the spoils equal to that of an ordinary buccaneer, despite the fact that the self-righteous Esquemeling declared one of them to be more deserving 'to be broken alive on the wheel' than offered such inducements.

At this point it appears to have occurred to Morgan that a full-scale attack on the fortress of San Lorenzo at the mouth of the Chagres river, just as much as an attack on Portobello, would be notified to Panama City and interpreted as a prelude to an attack on Panama itself. He therefore evolved the ruse of dispatching only a small part of his force to capture San Lorenzo, in the hope that this would arouse less apprehension that the attack was a prelude to something else. The capture of such a commanding fortress would have been a tough assignment for the whole 'army' of 1800 men; Captain Brodeley (probably Bradley), who was allocated only four ships and four hundred men, was none the less told to take the fortress, prevent the escape of messengers to Panama, and then hold the position until Morgan arrived with the main body of the buccaneer force. Morgan expected as much of his subordinates as he demanded of himself.

The castle of San Lorenzo (about which more will be said from personal observation in a later chapter) was – with good reason – considered well-nigh impregnable. It was built on a sugar-loaf hillock (*not* a 'high mountain' as Esquemeling has it) with the sea and the mouth of the Chagres lapping steep cliffs and banks on three sides; on the fourth there was a thirty-foot moat and a single drawbridge. There were gun terraces below the main fortress commanding the approach and entrance to the river. The walls were 'as secure as the best walls made of stone and brick', being constructed of strong wooden palisades filled with earth between them.

But it was these walls which the experienced Bradley ('this man had been a long time in those quarters, and committed many robberies upon the Spaniards') saw as the key to entry. As usual the buccaneers planned an overland attack. The guides from Old Providence led them from their landing-place, a few miles up the coast, through dense jungle to the landward walls of the fortress. But the Spaniards had observed the approach of Bradley's ships and were fully prepared for an overland attack. A strip of jungle on the far side of the moat had been cleared, and as the buccaneers emerged from the forest they came under a withering fire from the palisades – 'they being in an open place where nothing could cover nor defend them'.

The gun terrace of Fort San Lorenzo with the Chagres river in the background

Then occurred one of those improbably dashing incidents in which Esquemeling's narrative abounds. One of the buccaneers was shot by an arrow

which pierced his body to the other side. This instantly he pulled out with great valour at the side of his breast; then taking a little cotton that he had about him, he wound it round the said arrow, and putting it into his musket shot it back into the castle. But the cotton being kindled by the powder, occasioned two or three houses that were within the castle, being thatched with palm leaves, to take fire.

The fire spread; confusion followed within the fortress. Bradley then was able to implement the plan which he had devised: he piled brushwood against the palisades – now less heavily defended – and set fire to it. The fire caught the wooden walls of the palisades, and as these collapsed the earth fillings spilled out into a small ravine which formed a moat; soon the walls were practically down and the moat practically levelled up. The marauders fired into the fortress whenever they saw a target silhouetted against the flames. By dawn the following day the way was clear for the buccaneers to do what they were best at – effect a hand-to-hand assault with cutlass, pike and pistol. The Spanish governor was made of sterner stuff than his colleague at Old Providence: he rallied his men in the breaches and died where he stood. The rest of the garrison were soon slain or rounded up, but not before a few survivors had slipped away in the confusion to carry news of the invasion to Panama. Chagres had fallen, but surprise had been lost.

It had been a classic assault, bearing comparison – albeit on a miniature scale – with those to be executed a few years later in Europe by Louis de Vauban, the French master of fortress construction and also of siege techniques. Vauban's star-shaped citadels defied capture by reason of their enfilading fields of fire, each spoke of the star protecting its neighbour. His assault technique ('a city besieged by Vauban is a city taken', said Louis XIV) was to approach the walls by means of carefully sited slit-trenches and, when his artillery had weakened the fabric of the battlements, to fill in the moat with bundles of faggots carried forward up the slit-trenches for that purpose, and then eventually to rush the walls with pike and with that novel weapon the bayonet. Bradley was infinitely less sophisticated, but his principle was not dissimilar: he weakened the defences by fire power, infiltrated men with faggots to burn the wooden palisades and let the earth so released do the work of filling the moat; then the final frenzied assault.

With San Lorenzo in buccaneer hands, the way was now clear for Morgan to follow with the main body of his ships and men. As he sighted the English flag flying over the castle he appears to have allowed his enthusiasm to overcome his nautical good sense: he sailed his flagship – the *Satisfaction* – straight on to the reef which lay just below the surface off the mouth of the river.

The sharp coral bank, clearly visible from the height of the castle, was less visible from the deck of a ship. But common prudence should have dictated careful observation from the masthead, a measured approach and continual soundings. It was an inexcusable piece of bad seamanship. Three of Morgan's other vessels followed the *Satisfaction* on to the reef. All were total wrecks, but the crews got safely ashore. Esquemeling – whose censures on Morgan tend to be moral rather than professional – makes light of the affair:

> the joy of the whole fleet was so great when they spied the English colours upon the castle that they minded not their way into the river.

He hurries over the incident and goes on to describe at length the reception of Morgan at San Lorenzo. This was the second flagship Morgan had lost within three years, and was the last he was ever to have.

The losses to the buccaneers at the storming of San Lorenzo had been heavy, over a hundred killed and seventy wounded out of a total of 400; and Captain Bradley himself later died of his wounds. However, Morgan wasted little time before pressing on. He left a stay-behind party at San Lorenzo to repair the fort with the help of the surviving Spanish prisoners and to guard the ships, no doubt mindful of the disconcerting return from Villahermosa when his transport had been captured while he had been up-country, and of his even more alarming return from the lagoon of Maracaibo when his line of retreat had been blocked. Realizing that the Spaniards had been alerted to his intended line of advance, and confident that there would be ambushes set for him along the route, Morgan decided that it would be best to travel in fighting trim with a minimum encumbrance of rations: provisions would be captured as they overwhelmed the forces resisting their advance. This arrogant attitude towards the commissariat nearly proved fatal to the whole enterprise.

The voyage up the Chagres was grim. The river was low and

the boats constantly went aground. Portage was difficult along the swampy jungle banks. The expected ambuscades did not materialize, as the Spaniards retreated from one clearing after another, leaving burnt-out huts and smoking camp fires behind them. The buccaneers – as at Old Providence – reacted badly to hunger and discomfort; for fighting they were prepared, for starvation they were not. At one abandoned camp site they found a few old leather saddle-bags, which they shredded and shaved with their cutlasses before boiling and eating them. At another clearing in the jungle they found some stray cats which they ate. On the seventh day of their march without rations they overran a deserted village in which they unearthed 'fifteen or sixteen jars of Peru wine'. The effect of this on the empty stomachs of the troops was disastrous; Morgan was probably responsible for putting out a report that the wine was poisoned and should not be touched. The canoes were abandoned as the line of advance left the course of the river, and encounters with Indians – but not with Spaniards – became more frequent. Tropical storms not only soaked the hungry, feverish men but – more serious – dampened their powder and rusted their weapons; what huts they could find were used to shelter the firearms while the buccaneers alternately shivered or sweated in the steaming forests.

Eventually jungle gave way to savannah. A hill was climbed (another of Esquemeling's 'high mountains') from which they could – like stout Cortez upon a peak in Darien – spy the Southern (Pacific) Ocean. Ironically, the first thing they saw was the Spanish treasure ships sailing away from Panama to the safety of the off-shore islands. But the city itself was prize enough. Heartened by their view of their goal, the buccaneers pressed on until, on the tenth day since leaving San Lorenzo, they saw the Spanish army drawn up on the plains in front of the city barring their further advance.

If Morgan and his men were exhausted by physical privation and exertion, Don Juan Perez de Guzman, the Spanish President and Captain-general of the Audiencia of Panama, was exhausted by nervous strain. He had known for more than two

weeks that the English were advancing on his rich and –
physically at least – defenceless city. He had been shaken by the
news that the impregnable fortress of San Lorenzo had fallen to
frontal attack. He had made careful deployments for ambushes
along the route to be used by the intruders, but these had come
to naught because of the pusillanimity of his subordinates. He
had hoped that the rigours of the terrain and the scorched-earth
policy applied to the settlements along the English line of
advance would have caused them to turn back; yet now they
were reportedly almost at his gates. He had received alarming
reports of the numbers and ferocity of his assailants. No wonder
he had taken to his bed.

But now that the moment for decisive action had come, Don
Juan – a veteran of the wars in the Spanish Netherlands – rose
for and to the occasion. Knowing the inadequacy of his city's
fortifications, and realizing that the buccaneers were unused to
fighting against regular troops on an open battlefield, he sens-
ibly led his army of over 1200 infantry and about 400 cavalry out
to camp on the plains in front of the city. But his own resolution
was not matched by that of his men: during the night large
numbers slipped away from camp and returned to the psycho-
logically reassuring environment of the city. Don Juan was
obliged to return also to try to re-form and put some spirit into
his garrison. He attended a special service in the cathedral,
made an oath to die in defence of Our Lady of the Immaculate
Conception, and donated to her shrine a diamond ring worth
4000 pieces of eight. (All this he recorded as part of his military
preparations in his official dispatch to Madrid.) He then again
led his army out of the city to take up its definitive position for a
pitched battle with the buccaneers.

As well as a slight preponderance of troops, Don Juan had a
secret weapon on which he placed much store: he had rounded
up a herd of some thousands of head of cattle and planned to
drive them, at the crucial moment in the battle, into the ranks of
the invaders. The concept that somehow cattle might do the
work of cavalry was to prove as misconceived as it was in-
glorious; but it put some heart into the negroes, mulattos

and Indians – many of them slaves – who swelled the ranks of the imperial Spanish army.

The buccaneers, despite their weariness, had broken into uncontrolled cheering when first they saw the city of Panama stretched before them; they had filled their bellies with beef, slaughtered on the plains, after their long and hungry march (the Spaniards' scorched-earth policy having broken down just at the moment when it should have been most rigorously enforced); they were light-headed and elated at the prospect of action and plunder. But they too had reason for apprehension. The action that confronted them on 19 January 1671 was not a beach landing or an ambuscade, a sudden assault or a confused night attack: it was something of which neither they nor their 'admiral' commander had any previous experience – a formal, set-piece, seventeenth-century land battle, against a Spanish commander of continental European experience.

It has been said that the outcome of most battles is decided by the mistakes of the loser rather than by the skills of the victor. The battle of Panama was no exception. To start with, the site on which Don Juan drew up his army, although it had some superficial attractions – a ravine and hillock apparently protecting his right flank – did not give proper scope for his cavalry to manoeuvre: 'the field being full of quags and very soft underfoot, they could not ply to and fro and wheel about'. Furthermore, his artillery was sited in such a way that the wind blew the cannon smoke across the lines of the Spanish musketeers, reducing their fire capacity. Also – an important factor in a tropical afternoon battle – the Spaniards were drawn up with the sun in their eyes.

Don Juan had envisaged a frontal attack by the English; this would have been in keeping with their reputation and practice. But Morgan was too canny to charge the main body of Spanish cannon positioned in their centre. Studying the Spanish lines through his nautical spy-glass, he calculated that the same ravine which Don Juan was relying upon to protect his right flank would also hamper any efforts to reinforce that flank; he therefore decided to make his main thrust in this sector.

Captain (designated for the day 'Lieutenant-Colonel') Lawrence Prince led the English vanguard on foot; despite their obvious vulnerability to an enemy cavalry charge, Morgan had not provided his vanguard with pikes (which had never been a favourite buccaneer weapon on long jungle marches). It was nearly their undoing: Don Juan immediately dispatched a squadron of cavalry to cut short their advance, and Captain Prince only saved his force from annihilation by forming them into squares (a tactic not to become routine until more than a century later) and firing aimed shots into the mounted enemy swirling around them. As so often, the buccaneers' marksmanship ensured a heavy toll of Spanish horses and riders. The Spanish infantry, dispatched to follow up the cavalry, fared no better; when their repeated assaults did not allow the buccaneers time to reload their muskets, the latter resorted to their cutlasses – a weapon viewed by the rapier-carrying Spaniards as at once uncouth and terrifying.

While this engagement with Morgan's vanguard had been occupying the main attention of the Spanish viceroy, Captain Collier (commanding the English left wing) had taken advantage of dead ground to approach and capture the hillock on the right flank of the Spanish line. He now wheeled down the slope to relieve Prince and turn a Spanish withdrawal into what Morgan described as 'plain running'. Morgan for his part was occupied in attacking the Spanish left flank. So far, most of the aggressive initiatives had come from the English side. Now Don Juan deemed it was time to play his imagined trump card: the cattle stampede was ordered. As might have been predicted, the herds of bulls and oxen – distraught by the noise of gunfire and the smell of powder – proved to be a totally unguided missile; they were quickly headed off by the buccaneers and turned first on their own herdsmen and then on an unsuspecting company of Spanish infantry who happened to be in their path.

The person of the President and Captain-general was now the only hope of rallying the remnant of the imperial forces. Don Juan, as he subsequently reported, 'went forward to comply with my word to the Virgin to die in her defence', turning a deaf

The battle of Panama showing Don Juan's cattle stampede at the left foreground, from Esquemeling's English edition

ear to the twice-repeated urgings of his domestic chaplain that honour was satisfied and that he should withdraw from the mêlée; but at the third time of supplication, Don Juan succumbed to his chaplain's nervous entreaties that his action was 'mere desperation . . . and not like a Christian'. Captain-general and priest retired from the fray together, deciding that – in all the circumstances – 'it was a miracle of the Virgin to bring them off safely among so many thousand bullets'.

The pitched battle was over; the survivors of the Spanish army scampered as best they could back to the inadequate shelter of the buildings of Panama. Morgan's exultant buccaneers now advanced for a type of encounter with which they were more familiar: the sacking of a city. But even now, Panama was not entered and taken without further costly fighting, and shortly after it was finally subjugated a fire spread through the city destroying the rich merchants' residences, the well-stocked warehouses, many of the churches with their communion plate . . . everything, in fact, which the buccaneers had for so long been looking forward to ransacking. The origin of the fire – as is so often the case when cities are burnt in wars – remains obscure. Morgan in his dispatches to Modyford says that the viceroy 'commanded the city to be fired and its chief forts blown up'. Don Juan, on the other hand, in his retrospective dispatch already quoted above, says that the owners of the houses and their slaves set fire to them, but he gives no convincing reason why they should have done so. Popular report, both at the time and subsequently, attributed the fire to the buccaneers; the theory that they indulged in widespread arson out of spite seems improbable, as the flames and destruction must have much hindered looting; the possibility that the fire resulted from the excited excesses of the buccaneers seems much more likely. Morgan gathered his men together shortly after the city fell and cautioned them against the 'poisoned' wine they might find; he may well have been reacting to drunken destruction already perpetrated (although Esquemeling puts the warning before the fire in his narrative). Whatever the cause, Panama burnt.

There were further disappointments for the looters. One of the ships they had seen escaping towards the horizon when they first spied the city had, in fact, been carrying the bullion from the royal storehouses, which were now found to be empty. The great gold altar in one of the main churches, which was too heavy to remove, had been painted over to look like wood and thus avoided detection. Don Juan and some of his closest associates (doubtless including the chaplain with the highly developed sense of self-preservation) escaped to the hills.

But as the buccaneers intensified their hunt for valuables in the ruins of the city a certain amount came to hand. Wells and water cisterns were frequently found to contain hastily secreted plate and coin. Bands of buccaneers dispatched into the surrounding countryside brought in prisoners. Some of these, according to Esquemeling, 'were put to the most exquisite tortures imaginable' to tell where their own and the neighbours' valuables were concealed. Indeed, Esquemeling describes in nauseating detail the fate of one unfortunate lad who purloined his master's taffeta breeches in the general confusion and was unable to tell his captors the whereabouts of a casket for which he had a most promising-looking silver key in his pocket. Others among those rounded up, who seemed to be the families of people of substance, were held to ransom. Priests in particular were expected to disgorge well if they were to escape an application of their own racks and inquisition instruments. And yet, if all Esquemeling's horror tales are true, it is surprising that no one let on about the painted altar.

As for the fate of the women of Panama, Esquemeling devotes a long passage to describing how Morgan himself attempted to seduce a gentlewoman 'of good quality' and impeccable morals, first employing blandishments and then threats to induce her to succumb to his 'disorderly request'. The whole incident, with its direct reported speech ('Sir, my life is in your hands, but as to my body . . .' etc.) sounds inherently improbable and seems likely to be just another of Esquemeling's libels on Morgan. Other women undoubtedly suffered the traditional fate of those in sacked cities; Spanish complaints were vociferous and the buccaneers' protestations of innocence about as convincing as Lord Byron's on behalf of the ravishers of Ismail:

> But all the ladies, save some twenty score,
> Were almost as much virgins as before.

Morgan stayed about a month in all at Panama. Towards the end of this time he was beginning to have trouble with some of his own men, who were contemplating defecting with a captured ship and setting themselves up as pirates in the Pacific. He promptly had their ship dismasted. When eventually the homeward march began, the buccaneers took with them the remaining unredeemed hostages, threatening to carry them off to Jamaica if their ransoms were not paid. Then, with the booty loaded on to nearly two hundred mules, they set off back, by the same route as they had come, to the mouth of the Chagres river. The journey was very different from the outward one: this time there was plenty to eat, and the rains had swelled the river so that the canoes no longer went aground as on the former occasion.

But there were different problems. Relations between the buccaneers themselves were under strain: the 'purchase' had been less spectacular than they had hoped for from a city of fabled wealth, captured after such a gruelling campaign. There were rumours that some of the buccaneers, contrary to agreement and convention, had secreted gems and other small valuables about their persons, rather than contribute them to the common haul. Morgan therefore halted his march and ordered a body-search of the entire force. The French protested volubly, and Morgan only quieted them by subjecting himself to a public search to show that no stigma attached to the process.

The total value of the whole booty was estimated at 400,000 pieces of eight; but by the time the wounded had been compensated, the captains had received their own larger cuts, Morgan had received his one per cent, and King Charles and the Duke of York (as Lord High Admiral) had had their respective one-fifteenth and one-tenth shares set aside, the share-out to ordinary buccaneers amounted to a mere two hundred pieces of eight. This would have been about the price of only the most modest plot of land in Jamaica. There was much grumbling and – according to Esquemeling – accusations that Morgan had kept back more than his entitlement. The expedition broke up in bad order: Morgan returned to Jamaica with only four of the original ships' companies with him, and many of the rest went their separate – and often piratical – ways.

The population of Jamaica, however, had an unqualified welcome for the returning hero. He had once more brought riches – or, at least, much spending money – to the island, and had delivered a resounding rebuff to the Spanish would-be invaders. He was fêted in the taverns and retired honourably to his estates to write an account of his exploits. When this was completed, the island Council met and passed a resolution giving Morgan 'many thanks for executing his last commission, and approving very well of his acting therein'. Approbation could hardly have been more universal or explicit.

Few would have foretold that within a year Henry Morgan would have been travelling back to England under close arrest to await trial in London for his conduct of the Panama campaign. The London of Samuel Pepys and Christopher Wren, of Restoration comedy and Nell Gwynn was to prove more dangerous to Morgan than the jungles of the Chagres river or the charging bulls on the plains of Panama.

[8]

Crossing the Isthmus without Morgan

For anyone wishing to retrace Captain Morgan's march across the isthmus of Panama today there are two main problems, both of them nearly intractable.

Firstly, there is the fact that the geography has been tampered with. While the fifteen miles of the Chagres river nearest to its mouth remain almost untouched since the seventeenth century, further up the river its course becomes lost in a wilderness of watery lagoons caused by flooding following the cutting of the Panama Canal in the first decade of this century.

The second obstacle is that those lower reaches of the Chagres which are still intact are now virtually inaccessible. Their unspoilt nature is directly responsible for this: an area of virgin tropical forest in the vicinity of large US army bases (such as those installed in proximity to the Panama Canal) is invaluable as a jungle warfare training area, and consequently the whole region surrounding both banks of the Chagres has been so designated. Any idea that I could hire a little boat and set off on my own up the river, or that I could make a parallel march up its banks under my own steam, was immediately dispelled by our well-informed ambassador in Panama City. Perhaps, he suggested, I would like to hear straight from the horse's mouth just how impossible my ideas were? He would be very pleased to arrange an interview for me with the general commanding the US southern army group, whose headquarters were in the former Canal Zone of Panama.

Everything about the general was a little larger than life-size. His headquarters were like a small town, his office had the dimensions of a tennis court, his desk the proportions of a billiard table; his dog was a Great Dane; and when the general himself got up from his chair he seemed to go on rising for a remarkably long time before he reached his six foot nine inches (in combat boots). His handshake should be shunned by concert pianists and others with a requirement for retaining any sensation in their fingers.

The general asked me about Cuba and I asked him about the defence of the Canal. We talked about Latin American politics and politicians, about guerrilla warfare in Malaya and in Vietnam, about disarmament and rearmament . . . about everything, in fact, except what was on my mind: how to penetrate the banks of the Chagres river. At last he gave me an opening to make some enquiries.

'And what brings you to this part of the world, Mr Ambassador?'

I explained about Morgan and the inaccessibility of the Chagres.

'Inaccessibility is a relative term, Mr Ambassador. How would you like to see your river? What about a chopper? Quarter of an hour and you could see the whole length of it . . . go as low as you like . . . monkey's eye view – that's what I call it.'

'You're very kind, General; but Henry Morgan sweated it out in a boat and then on foot, and that's really what I had in mind, but I gather it's a no-go area now.'

'It's true that the banks of the Chagres are normally a closed area, but it would always be useful to us to hear some comparisons between this jungle and that which you knew as a veteran of the Malayan Emergency.' (Could that steely grey eye have a mocking twinkle in it?) 'Only thing is, I'd hate you to get lost or eaten. There are no paths in that forest and some fairly unfriendly mammals, reptiles and insects. Every time I've been there I've come away feeling that that chap Noah was altogether too comprehensive in drawing up his passenger list. Can't let you go alone, but tell you what I'll do. The commander of Port Sherman has a Ranger unit on his strength. Those chaps have come all the way from Texas so as to get their jungle boots worked in. They'd just love the excuse to go up that river of yours.'

The next day I was driving a small hired car across the peninsula to Fort Sherman on the Caribbean coast of Panama. There are surprises for the motorist on the highway: one is unconscious of the fact that the road is following the Canal until suddenly a ship the size of a factory looms up alongside, or where one had expected a traffic light one finds a lighthouse. I decided to make a diversion on the way to Fort Sherman; just before the village of Cativa, I turned north-east; soon the road gave out and I was on the rough track, running parallel with the coast and fringed with banana groves, that led to Portobello – the scene of the assault by Morgan on the expedition two years before his Panama venture. What Morgan did there, how Thomas Gage had earlier found the town and how I had later done so has already been described in an earlier chapter.

After this brief interlude, I drove back westwards along the road heading for Fort Sherman and my Ranger guide for the Chagres. I skirted the Caribbean terminal of the Canal at Colón – a town which amounts to the biggest duty-free shop in the world – and crossed the Canal itself for the first time by the lock gates at Gatun.

The necessity of locks was bitterly contested by the builders of the Panama Canal. The original French project, launched and directed by Ferdinand de Lesseps of Suez Canal fame, was for a sea-level canal. He and his team of engineers in the 1880s concentrated in the first place on digging the 'cut' at Culebra and trying to control the rise and fall of the Chagres river. Both problems were bedevilled by the same aspect of the climate which had so dampened the spirits of Morgan and his men: the phenomenal rainfall. However deep the Culebra Cut was dug, the rain would wash the banks down into it. Equally, there was no way of stabilizing or damming the Chagres river which would control rises frequently of ten feet a day and – exceptionally, as in October 1885 – of thirty feet in a few hours. One of de Lesseps' assistants described his voyage down the flooded

Chagres as 'gliding past half-drowned trees the tops of which were black with millions of tarantulas'.

But as I peered along the line of the Canal I recalled that it was not the difficulty of the engineering feats but the toll of lost lives which eventually crippled the French project. This had always been a notoriously fever-ridden isthmus: the early Spanish settlers and those who preyed on them – including Drake and Morgan – had their casualties from disease; but it was not until the building of the railway across the isthmus in the mid-nineteenth century that the full enormity of the health hazard was recognized. As with other railways since, it was said that every sleeper had cost a human life. 'Chagres fever' – almost certainly yellow fever, which had first appeared in the West Indies in 1647 – and malaria were the great killers; bodies were shipped out and sold to medical schools all over the world (the Company claimed to have built hospitals with the proceeds). The French Canal Company inherited these medical problems.

De Lesseps – 'the Great Undertaker' as he came to be called – fought the evidence rather than the disease: he went on maintaining as long as he could that there were 'only a few cases [of yellow fever] brought in from abroad'. But the figures could not be suppressed for ever. In 1883 there were 420 recorded deaths among the Canal employees, but as these only took account of those who died in hospital, and most of the sick – because of the cost – never went near a hospital, the real losses were probably three times as many. In 1884 deaths of workers rose to 200 a month. By 1885 it was reckoned that of every four who came out from France, two or even three died; and out of one group of 33 Italian labourers who arrived that year 27 were dead within three weeks. These were proportional casualties not to be matched until the trench warfare of Flanders. The bodies of black workers were often shovelled into the waste earth removed from the Cut as the only form of burial available. Nor was it only the labourers who died like flies: of 24 nursing sisters – known on account of their white winged headdresses as 'God's Geese' – only two survived; and the local director-general of the project (de Lesseps himself remained in Paris) lost in turn his daughter, his son, his daughter's companion and his wife. Ships in Colón harbour bobbed about at their anchors without a living soul on board, their crews annihilated by the dreadful fever. Even in Panama City itself conditions were not much better; indeed, so insanitary was the town that when Paul Gauguin (who had temporarily abandoned his painting to earn some money working on the Canal) was arrested for urinating in the main square, he defended himself on the grounds that the whole town was one open sewer!

As I waited for the lock gates to open, and wondered whether there would be a toll fee to pay, I ruminated on the other great scandal of the French canal project: the financial one. While the personnel had been dying as if smitten by a medieval plague, the survivors had kept their spirits up by conventionally French means: the consumption of champagne at Colón during the 1880s was greater *per capita* than in any city of the Western hemisphere; the fact that wine was indisputably safer to drink than the local water was a much quoted justification. A visiting journalist reported that, after coffin-making, the most prosperous local industries were gambling houses and brothels. Salaries and expense accounts for the executives of the company were – and had to be – enormous. When eventually de Lesseps conceded that he had to abandon the idea of a sea-level canal and build locks, he hired the foremost civil engineer of France, no less a person than Gustave Eiffel, fresh from the glory of completing his tower, to supervise the work at Gatun. All this required vast sums of capital to be raised from French private investors. A public lottery was introduced; share prospectuses were less than frank. When eventually the crash came and work had to be abandoned there were many embarrassing questions left unanswered; it was several years before investigations revealed the extent of the deception, and criminal charges were brought. Ferdinand de Lesseps was deemed too old and sick to stand trial, but his son was convicted and even Monsieur Eiffel was sentenced to two years in gaol for his share in the financial frauds. At this point, at the end of the last century, it looked as if a Panama Canal would never be constructed.

The lock gates had opened and I drove through to the western side of the Canal, turning almost immediately north and following the road through a region of scrub and training camps which led after ten miles to the US army base at the north-western tip of Limon Bay; this bore the proud name of Fort Sherman. It revealed itself as a complex of barracks, parade grounds, assault courses, check points, flag poles, sandbags, fire buckets and all the universally recognizable clobber of military life.

I had been told by the general in Panama City to ask for Major Stein; the major turned out to be built by the same firm who had constructed the general; he loomed above me in even larger combat boots, doing a lot of saluting and very little speaking. I was plied with Coke and assurances of cooperation. Senior Sergeant Chuck Cherry, his best jungle instructor and himself a veteran of Vietnam, would escort me up the Chagres, across the Gatun Lake and down the Las Cruces Trail to Old Panama. He had a Boston Whaler and the plan was that I should go with him round the coast from Fort Sherman (the modern camp – a 'fort' in name only) to Fort San Lorenzo (the old citadel, still very recognizable as the fort which Bradley had assaulted) at the mouth of the Chagres river. We would thus approach exactly as Morgan had done, across the coral reef, sailing directly inshore towards the prominent headland commanding the entrance to the wide river.

My first sight of Sgt Cherry the following day was a surprise. I had been expecting another military giant. Instead, when I looked down the path to the waterfront where he was waiting for me in the Boston Whaler, I saw a slight, wiry man with circular steel-rimmed spectacles.

'Mind how you come down, Mr 'bassador, Sir. There are a hundred and thirty-eight steps.'

'Thank you, Sergeant,' I said, vaguely wondering whether I was meant to count them on the steep descent.

The two-man boat, with its powerful inboard motor, was loaded with provisions and jerry-cans of petrol. It was not long before we were chugging our way towards Fort Lorenzo. This had always been a dangerous stretch of coast for the Spaniards, because the small river boats plying between the mouth of the Chagres and Portobello had been easy prey to raiders. When Thomas Gage made the trip in 1637 on his way from Old Panama to Portobello (the reverse of our own trip) he reported that his ship mounted an all-night watch for fear of Dutch privateers, and that they were all relieved when dawn broke without incident. Gage's description of the whole journey, which was published in England in 1648 and was available to Morgan, had doubtless been a major factor in encouraging him to undertake the Panama venture at all: there was much in Gage to incite daring and provoke cupidity. He recounts that the defences along the Chagres had been allowed to fall into disrepair because the Spaniards were convinced that the currents and shallows of the river were in themselves sufficient to prevent invaders reaching Venta de Cruz by water. Thereafter he described the Las Cruces Trail as 'for the most part flat . . . and very agreeable'. Finally, Old Panama itself had all its artillery facing seaward (like Singapore in 1942) and was 'much given to sin, looseness . . . and lust'.

For part of the nine miles of coastline, the shore was steeply cliff-faced; we kept our distance from the rocks at its foot. At other points, the shore was gentler; woods rose from small beaches. It would have been at one of these that Captain Bradley had disembarked his men to start their march to the landward side of Fort Lorenzo. We pressed on, making little effort at conversation above the noise of the motor, until Sgt Cherry volunteered:

'Never met an ambassador before. When I heard you were coming I did some *re*search. Did you know there are 3,920 ambassadors altogether in the world? Thought you'd like to know. Bet not many of you know the number.'

'I'm sure not. How fascinating . . .' But before I could enquire the source of this esoteric information he had focused his attention on something else:

'You see that hill? That's San Lorenzo. Behind it you'll see the entrance to the Chagres.'

We did a sweep out to sea but failed to locate the submarine reef on which Morgan had lost his flagship, and then we came in close under the sheer cliff sides of the old fort. The gun terraces at sea-level were clearly discernible. We landed on the sheltered riverward side of the fort and clambered upwards among young saplings and dense thorns. In no way could such an approach have been made if the fortress above us had been manned by hostile defenders. When eventually we emerged we found ourselves at the bottom of that ravine which had formed a natural moat between the defenders' palisade and the landward approach to the fort – in that moat, in fact, which the buccaneers had partially filled with brushwood before their final assault on the burning palisades.

Emerging from the moat, we found the ground plan of the fort still fairly intelligible. There were rows of ancient cannon pointing both towards the land and towards the sea. The view up the river was a commanding one: nothing could have proceeded upstream against the wishes of the *castellan* of San Lorenzo. Looking seaward one could clearly discern a broken line of darker water, with occasional ripples; this must have been the danger signal of a hidden reef, so clear to Captain Bradley's men on the parapets and so unclear to Admiral Morgan's men on the poop of *Satisfaction*.

Sgt Cherry followed the line of my gaze.

'Did you know there had been an average of one and a quarter ships wrecked off this coast every year since the Panama Canal was built?'

'My goodness, what a lot.'

'No, Sir. *Before* the Canal was built it was running at one and three-quarters. Sort of interesting. Thought you'd want to know.'

Once again, before I could question all this random erudition, my informant had moved on; this time he had turned on his heels and started the descent to the Boston Whaler.

Now we began our progress up the Chagres itself. Here at its mouth it was a wide and fairly tranquil stretch of water, and I was to discover that it kept these characteristics right up to Gatun Lock, fifteen miles away. Since the permanent flooding

of vast areas in the centre of the Panama peninsula, there have
no longer been the rapid and unpredictable rises of water which
so disconcerted the early canal builders. No longer do trees
disappear leaving only their tops – black with tarantulas – above
the muddy waters.

But this relative tranquillity did not mean that the river was
monotonous. As we ascended it, each change of direction
brought a fresh vista of huge trees lining the banks and of tiny
creeks penetrating into the jungle on either side. For some

Up the Chagres with the US Rangers

while we kept to the middle of the river. At this point Morgan would have had little difficulty in keeping his canoes afloat; it was only as they ascended further that their bottoms would have started to grate on unsuspected sandbanks and to get snagged in the fallen trees at the water's edge.

Sgt Cherry read my thoughts:

'It might be more interesting to explore one of those side streams for a while. I always tell my recruits that it's only when the jungle meets over your head, and you have to have a man in the bows with a machete, and creepers tangle in your hair, and thorns rip your clothing and your arms, and you can smell the rotting undergrowth that you begin to get the feel of the thing. But I keep forgetting – you're a jungle veteran yourself, Sir.'

I looked up quickly but could catch no glimpse of mockery behind the glinting glasses.

We agreed to take the Whaler up the next promising creek. The one we chose started well enough. It even turned south-east, parallel to the main line of the river. But soon we were in difficulties.

'Can't risk this weed getting into my motor,' announced Cherry. 'If you want to go any further we'll have to land and see what the going's like on foot.'

'Why not? After all, it's what Henry Morgan had to do a lot of the way.'

We tied up to a tangle of branches and creepers that overhung the dark brown water, and jumped ashore. Four paces into the forest and we were out of sight of the Whaler. Cherry – a professional to the tips of his jungle boots – was already checking his bearing from a prismatic compass.

We marched in silence between the bank of our tributary stream and the main river; thus it was that Morgan's thousand men must have progressed after the canoes began to run aground. I had forgotten how noisy the jungle could be: monkeys chattered above us; frogs croaked warning of our approach; rotting branches creaked and sometimes snapped; there was the hum of insect life. At dusk all this cacophony of sound would – I remembered – crescendo to a point at which it was quite difficult to hear people talking only a few yards away, and impossible to hear the stealthy approach of an enemy.

Every few minutes Sgt Cherry would stop, bend down and flick one or two leeches off his boots or trousers; I did the same. Caught like this, before they had fastened on flesh, they were slim, inch-long, caterpillar-like black objects, with a remarkable ability to climb by a series of jack-knife-like motions. Once they had climbed above the defences (boots with sewn-in tongues, etc.) and penetrated one's clothing, they soon found bare flesh on which to settle; then the leeches would quietly swell with the blood they sucked until they became a dark mound the size of a 5p or quarter dollar-coin; sometimes, if left unmolested (as they might well be, since they caused no pain) they would swell to far larger proportions. At this stage it would be too late to flick at them; their heads would be buried in one's flesh and remain there, even if their bodies were knocked off, to fester into jungle sores. There were, I recalled, two efficient expedients for persuading a grazing leech to look up from its dinner; one was a salt tablet, the other a lighted cigarette. Either of them applied lightly to the leech produced instant with-drawal symptoms; then a quick flick would send it rolling off replete, leaving only a harmless trickle of blood behind on one's leg or thigh. I wondered how many of Morgan's buccaneers had known how to cope; salt tablets and cigarettes they would not have had, and the matches for their flint-locks must have been too precious to use on something which was an irritant rather than a danger. Perhaps they used pieces of salted meat; Es-quemeling does not say. Sgt Cherry was a salt tablet man; he lent some to me.

'Don't use them all on the leeches,' he said. 'You'll need to swallow some to compensate for all the sweating you'll do before you reach Old Panama.'

It was indeed heavy going keeping parallel with the river. In the Malayan jungle it had been a maxim that a riverbank with a path along it was likely to be ambushed and therefore too dangerous a route to follow, and that a riverbank without a path along it was the thickest part of the forest and therefore an impractical route to follow. Cherry kept his distance from the bank – some thirty yards – and regularly halted our advance to make a lateral probe to the river to ensure that we had not lost it. Was this how Morgan had covered the ground? I doubted it. The banks of the Chagres would have been a more frequented highway in his day than in ours, and he would probably have found paths to follow. We know he did not fear ambush, but was hoping for a confrontation which would have enabled his men to capture rations from their Spanish assailants. Yet Esquemeling reports that for part of the way they too were hacking a path.

Even among connoisseurs of tropical rain forests, the jungle banks of the Chagres have always had a bad reputation. In that period when the Americans had taken over – after an interval – from the French the task of attempting to construct a Panama Canal, a poem appeared entitled 'Panama Patchwork' written by the self-appointed minstrel of the canal workers, James Stanley Gilbert:

> Beyond the Chagres River
>   'Tis said – the story's old –
> Are paths that lead to mountains
>   Of purest virgin gold;
> But 'tis my firm conviction,
>   Whatever tales they tell,
> That beyond the Chagres River
>   All paths lead straight to hell!

When Sgt Cherry decided it was time for a rest and a smoke (perhaps he had run out of salt tablets for his leeches?) I recited these lines to him.

'Do you know how many men died when we were building this Canal?' I was discovering that Sgt Cherry's comments usually took the form of questions; as usual, I was inadequate to the challenge.

'Nor do I,' came the unexpected comment. 'But it must have been like a battlefield.'

Despite the lack of this particular statistic, Cherry had clearly made a considerable study of 'the American period' in the building of the Canal – the years 1904 to 1914, when the United States had picked up and persevered with the project which the French had been obliged to abandon. He saw it, with some justification, as a story of personalities. And the chief among these was his hero, President Teddy Roosevelt, the driving force behind the whole enterprise. Cherry looked on Roosevelt as an honorary Ranger on account of his early days with the Rough Riders in Cuba and of his propensity – even in late middle age – to engage in para-military games.

'Do you know how he used to amuse his guests after lunch at the White House?' Scarcely waiting for my usual confession of ignorance, he pressed on: 'Assault courses! He'd take them on a walk round the grounds and they had to go over or through every obstruction in their path – fences, hedges, kennels, ponds. "Obstacle walks", he called them. Guess it sorted out the guests.'

I guessed it did.

'Do you know why he used to slip out in the middle of state banquets at the White House, and come back all ruffled?'

'He had a girl friend upstairs?' I hazarded.

Sgt Cherry looked shocked: 'No, Sir. Not so. He went up for a pillow fight in the nursery with his children; that's what he used to do. Used to come downstairs all covered in feathers sometimes.' He recited these feats of prowess almost as if they had been Ranger battle honours to which he had been witness.

But Cherry's interest in the Canal was not entirely restricted to the quirks of Teddy Roosevelt. He told me that many workers had died of yellow fever, many of dysentery, smallpox and malaria. He told me of the scare of bubonic plague, and of the rats – the size of guinea-pigs – who were found to be spreading it in Panama City. He explained how the black labourers had been paid in silver, and the white managerial employees in gold, and how the death rate from disease had been four times greater on the 'silver roll' than on the 'gold roll'. He told me how Teddy Roosevelt and the US government had encouraged the secession of Panama from Colombia in 1903, and of the cruel irony that when eventually the Canal was opened in August 1914 the event was completely overshadowed by the outbreak of the First World War in the same month. Every statement was preceded by a question and followed by a rapid display of facts, dates and – even more – figures. It was like conversing with the *Guinness Book of Records*.

It was time we returned to the Boston Whaler and continued our voyage up the Chagres. The river in its present form ends at Gatun Lock; thereafter it is lost in Gatun Lake – an area of 164 square miles (the size of Barbados, *not* – for once – of Wales) artificially flooded by the Canal makers. The Whaler had to be briefly transported (there were Rangers at the Lock) and put in the water again for the long chug across the open expanse of blue, jungle-fringed water. Before the flooding, this had been the infamous Black Swamp which had been said to be bottomless but which had been found, during the Canal excavations, to be in fact 185 feet of mud. Now, the swamp submerged forever, it looked like clear and inviting water.

As we crossed it we got glimpses of the railway line – built on a causeway for much of its route – which had been constructed (in its original form) in the mid-nineteenth century. De Lesseps had first reconnoitred the line of his projected canal by crossing the isthmus by rail. Even before the flooding of the region, it had been 'a half-drowned country': de Lesseps had noted that the 47½ miles of railway line had crossed 170 bridges and culverts of more than fifteen feet width and 134 of less. Morgan and his men had squelched through this sodden terrain; we skimmed over its surface.

But before long we were once again travelling exactly as the buccaneers had done. Near Gamboa we landed (the Whaler was collected by other Rangers) not far from the northern end of the Las Cruces Trail, which was the final part of Morgan's route. By the time they reached this point the buccaneers were in bad shape indeed. In the preceding days, while they found one ambush position and camp after another abandoned at their approach, they had got progressively nearer starvation: this was the period of eating leather bags and stray cats. It was not easy to pick up the start of the trail, and by the time we had done so the day was already nearly over. We had only gone two or three miles down it when suddenly it became too dark for further progress. There were fifteen miles ahead of us to Old Panama.

Sgt Cherry's jungle training equipment – though he was now outside the designated training area around the banks of the Chagres – came into its own. We had each been carrying one rubberized poncho cape; we laced up the hole (through which the owner would put his head when wearing it) and used one of them as a groundsheet, while attaching the other to branches and stakes to make a tent roof above our heads. We boiled a mess-tin of brackish water on a tiny ring of solid fuel, and poured into it various dehydrated packets to make up a warm and presumably nourishing stew. It tasted of nothing at all. Finally, from the top poncho we suspended two mosquito nets, tucking the bottoms of them in around us on the ground. Even when the inevitable rain came down we were reasonably dry and protected against all that crawled and crept through the decomposing leaves that made up the forest floor.

Sgt Cherry seemed subdued. He had not posed a factual question during all the time we had been pitching camp, and had not quoted a statistic since mid-afternoon. I felt he needed a little encouragement.

'I've been very lucky to have a companion on this trip who's so well informed. I don't know how you remember so many facts and figures,' I said. 'Some of them will come in very handy in my book.'

'Do you want to know why I ask questions? It's like this. My dad was a farmhand in up-state New York. Guess he drank a bit much. Specially after my mother died when we kids were all under five. So I never got much schooling – not proper schooling anyway. Everyone called me ignorant. I got right tired of it. So I thought I'd show them I knew more than all those school-taught kids and college boys. I just learnt the facts. You don't need theories if you know the facts. I collected reference books, almanacs, yearbooks . . . now I've got a whole library in my room. When they treated me like I was plain ignorant, I'd just think to myself "I wonder if Mr Clever-boots knows this or that?" So I started asking them questions which I knew the answers to. Made me feel much more comfortable when I found out they were more ignorant than me. So guess it's a habit now. Do you know how many questions I ask some days?'

As I rolled over to sleep I hoped that my own profound ignorance of so very many facts had done something to bolster the morale of this encyclopedic sergeant.

The following day we were up early for a rehydrated breakfast, and – after ruefully inspecting evidence on wrists and ankles of the mosquitoes which had managed to penetrate our defences – we set off confidently down the trail.

Our confidence was short-lived. Even the indomitable Cherry was daunted by the need to make an early detour round a 200-yard-wide swamp; having made the detour it was difficult to pick up the trail again with any real certainty that we were on the proper track. Great therefore was our relief when, a few miles on, we found substantial traces of paving: a strip some two yards wide and seventy yards long of well-worn, rough cobbles embedded in the mud and leaf-mould. It was Francisco Pizarro, before he sailed from Panama for his conquest of Peru in the sixteenth century, who had originally ordered the paving of the trail. It was reassuring to find traces of what it must have been like in its heyday. When had that heyday been?

The trail which we were now following had been at least a century old when Morgan trod it: it had been well established before Sir Francis Drake laid his ambush on it in 1573. It was to endure as a well-frequented trail for several centuries after Morgan too. But there were few years when it was as actively used as in 1849. That was the year of the gold rush in California. Many of the Forty-niners came from the cities of the eastern seaboard of the United States. There were only three ways in which they could get to the western gold fields: by waggon across the prairies, by sailing around Cape Horn, or by sea to Colón and then on foot across the isthmus to Panama City and the short sea passage to California. All three routes had their

drawbacks: the prairie crossing was liable to waggon break-
downs or attacks by Indians; the Cape route was liable to certain
seasickness and occasional shipwreck (it was also very expensive); and the isthmus crossing involved walking the Las Cruces
Trail. Local inhabitants of any standing rode the trail on horse
or muleback; but – almost by definition – the Forty-niners had
meagre or non-existent resources and had to go on foot. Many
faltered or collapsed on the way. One of them recorded count-
ing forty dead mules by the wayside. Another – a Massachusetts
man – is quoted by David McCullough (the historian of the
Panama Canal) as writing home saying:

> For no consideration take this route. I have nothing to say on
> the other routes, but do *not* take this one.

Cholera and yellow fever took a heavier toll of Forty-niners than
either the Cherokee Indians or the tempests round Cape Horn.

It was not only gold diggers who used the Las Cruces Trail at
that time to go from the east coast to the west coast of the United
States. In 1852, when the US 4th Infantry was posted to garrison
duty in California, several hundred soldiers of the regiment
together with their families made the crossing by this route. 150
men, women and children died in the course of the journey.
'The horrors of the road in the rainy season are beyond description', wrote the young captain in charge of one party. It was not
to be his last difficult military assignment. His name was
Ulysses S. Grant.

But in the hundred and thirty odd years since then, the trail
has fallen into ever worse condition. First the railway, then the
Canal and the good (military) motor roads across the isthmus
deprived it of traffic. Now it was so overgrown that there could
be no question of getting a mule along it; indeed, Sgt Cherry's
machete was in fairly regular use.

Not all the trail was through forests. There were stretches in
open savannah country. There were also innumerable small
rivers to cross which we tried to identify: the Cabulla, the
Casaya, or other nameless tributaries of the Chagres? There

were places which had clearly been traditional halts on the trail: small clearings where a quiet rummage in the undergrowth was more likely to produce the camping litter of the seventeenth or eighteenth centuries than of the twentieth – quaint old green bottles, mule's shoes, brass buttons.

Apart from the rivers which intersected it, there were other interruptions to progress along the trail. Deep gullies had to be slithered down and scrambled up. In one of these Morgan had lost three men killed and seven wounded in an ambush by the Indians. And at least three times we crossed more modern roads, one of which – a former military highway – ran parallel with the path for some quarter of a mile and effectively obliterated it in so doing. This was the only point in the eighteen miles where we consciously abandoned our trail.

It was at a point some six miles down our route, where the forest was particularly thick, that I calculated we must have reached the scene of Drake's celebrated ambush. He had in fact retraced his steps to this spot, after almost reaching Old Panama, when he had heard the glad tidings that the Treasurer of Lima was making the journey across the isthmus with his personal fortune before embarking for the voyage home to Spain. Like most diligent Spanish imperial officials, this dignitary had not neglected to line his own purse: his cabin luggage consisted of eight mule-loads of gold and one mule-load of jewels – enough to ensure a reasonably comfortable retirement for himself and an adequate dowry for the daughter who was accompanying him. Drake planned a night ambush in this advantageous place, and so that his own small party should not shoot at each other in the expected confusion of the attack, they are reported to have worn white shirts over their doublets. (How they managed to produce clean linen in the jungle swamps of the isthmus is not recorded.) The white shirts proved fatal to the success of the enterprise. One rather drunken seaman – a certain Robert Pike – lurched into the path of some mules coming the other way. A frightened rider warned the Treasurer of a ghostly figure on the trail, and that cautious official decided not to proceed further. Drake was frustrated,

The cathedral tower of Old Panama, in which the Spanish took
refuge from Morgan's attack

but philosophically concluded that perhaps the Treasurer's
personal treasure had been honestly come by and that it was no
part of the Almighty's purposes that the worthy man should be
parted from it. Henry Morgan, a century later, would have been
unmoved by such considerations.

The day wore on with more detours around swamps, more
gullies to clamber over, more insistent leeches, and more
questions from Sgt Cherry. I was unable to calculate where
might have been the tall tree up which Drake had climbed with
his Cimarron guides so that they could give him a view of the
Caribbean behind and his first view of the Pacific Ocean in
front. But before evening Sgt Cherry and I stood on a ridge in
open scrub country and could see Old Panama and the Pacific
just as Morgan's men had done. It would have been here that

the buccaneers slaughtered the cattle left behind by the Spaniards and alleviated their distressing hunger. Now it was all
downhill, and we did not have any Don Juan with an army of
Spaniards, Indians and bulls drawn up between us and our
destination.

The trail became overlaid with modern paths; fences diverted
us from our direct line of approach; the last mile or two of our
route was a confused anticlimax. But not so Old Panama itself.
The town which Morgan had – or had not – burnt, and which
had never been rebuilt on the same site, had grassed over until it
resembled a gentleman's park in which a number of Follies
protruded from the green swath.

Chief among these were the two great ecclesiastical monu-
ments of the old Spanish colonial city: the Convent of San
Francisco and the cathedral. These stone buildings had with-
stood the fire better than the wooden temporal structures. The
ornamental arched doorway of the convent, through which the
terrified wives and children of the defected Spanish garrison
had jostled in their rush for sanctuary, stood elegantly among its
ferns and moss like a backdrop for some sombre opera. The tall,
square tower of the cathedral, into which other refugees from
the advancing buccaneers had packed in their panic, stood
flanked by palm trees like the remnant of some crusader castle.

I had arrived: the Chagres river had been navigated; the Las
Cruces Trail trodden; the isthmus traversed from San Lorenzo
to Old Panama. Not for me the wild jubilation of Morgan's men
who had suffered so much and fought so hard to reach this
point, but I felt that some modest celebration was called for. I
went in search of Sgt Cherry and found him wandering among
the broken masonry scattered over the smooth turf which now
covered the site.

'Let's try to get a lift into Panama City proper,' I said. 'We've
earned a better meal than army packets and a drink that doesn't
need water-sterilizing tablets in it. I think with a bit of luck the
Embassy might give us a hot bath and lend us a couple of clean
shirts before we go out on the town.'

'I'm afraid I won't have time for that, Mr 'bassador. I have to get back by the train tonight; they're picking me up from Colón and driving me back to Fort Sherman. I have to be there by 10 p.m.'

'I'm really sorry,' I said – and meant it. 'But surely you've not got any duties tonight?'

'Duties? Oh goodness, no. It's the semi-finals of the US forces quiz on the radio. Those questions . . . they're real stiff. But you know I often do better than some of the competitors, and one day . . .'

A far-away look came into Cherry's eyes, and was still there when I bade him a grateful farewell.

9

Fortune's Wheel: Prisoner to Governor

Although Admiral Morgan had returned to a hero's welcome at Port Royal in April 1671 after his Panama adventure, the writing had in fact been on the wall for the buccaneers since 18 July 1670. It was on that date that Sir William Godolphin, British Ambassador at the court of Spain, had signed a peace treaty under which the Spanish conceded British ownership of those lands which the British occupied in the New World – explicitly including Jamaica – in return for a cessation of hostilities against Spanish possessions and shipping. It had been agreed in Madrid that the treaty would come into force a year to the day after it was signed; this time-gap was felt to be sufficient to ensure that every corner of the New World would be informed of the terms of the treaty before they became operative. But naturally it was assumed that forthwith both sides would cease to embark on deliberate provocations against the other.

By late May 1671, Sir Thomas Modyford as Governor of Jamaica still had no official notification of the treaty. Morgan had been home for a couple of months, and had already received the thanks of the Council of the Island, when the first formal communication about the outbreak of peace arrived – and it arrived not from London but from the Spanish governor of Puerto Rico. Modyford realized that he was in trouble and immediately set about writing a dispatch to Lord Arlington in London, justifying what Morgan had been allowed to do and claiming no knowledge at the time of the peace treaty with Spain. He was too late with his explanations. Within three weeks Sir Thomas Lynch landed from the frigate *Assistance* at Port Royal bringing with him the King's commission as lieutenant governor of Jamaica.

Enough was known in Jamaica about Lynch to make it clear to one and all that his appointment heralded a pacifist policy. However, there was a nominal vacancy for the post of lieutenant (deputy) governor, and it did not at first seem that Lynch's appointment affected Modyford's position as governor. Indeed, Modyford invited the Lynches to stay at King's House and treated them as honoured guests until their own residence could be furnished. But Modyford was harbouring a snake in the grass: unknown to him, Lynch had in his luggage another commission ordering him to arrest Modyford and take charge of the government of the island himself. He was biding his time until he calculated he could execute this order without provoking a riot. And while he waited to pounce, he continued to enjoy Modyford's hospitality in a manner not dissimilar to that in which Campbell of Glenlyon was to enjoy the MacDonalds' hospitality at Glencoe just twenty-one years later.

The reason for Lynch's orders was that Charles II and Lord Arlington had already got wind of Morgan's expedition against Panama, in advance of Modyford's dispatches, and they feared a sharp reaction from Spain. Lynch for his part was so nervous about the repercussions in Port Royal of any move against the popular Modyford that he decided the arrest could most safely be staged on board the *Assistance*. After several weeks, he lured Modyford on to the ship and sprang the trap. Modyford was sent home as a prisoner of state to be committed to the Tower, and Lynch ruled Jamaica alone.

This was an uncomfortable situation for Morgan, who was the active arm of Modyford's repudiated policy of defending Jamaica by assaulting the Spaniards before they could launch an attack. He persuaded the island's Council to send a resolution to London (it went by the same ship as Modyford) reaffirming that Morgan had acted at Panama with their commission. But when the full horrors of that campaign began to circulate in Madrid and London, no amount of retrospective justification could protect him. The Spanish Ambassador at the Court of St

James's was calling for Morgan's blood. Had not Panama been sacked six months after the peace treaty had been signed? Predictably, the next set of orders to reach Lynch instructed him also to arrest and send home Henry Morgan.

The admiral of the brethren of the coast was packed on board a leaking, ancient frigate – ironically named the *Welcome* – which had earlier been sunk and salvaged, and dispatched to Spithead in company with a condemned pirate. The confined conditions of a prisoner's cabin, the unaccustomed cold of the North Atlantic and the privations of a three-month voyage combined to result in Morgan arriving in England – to all outward appearances – a sick and broken man. He was not committed to the Tower like Modyford, but allowed to find his own lodgings in London providing he remained at the disposal of the authorities. It was not a happy home-coming to a native country which he had not seen since he left it, as a boy, in the bleak days of Cromwell's Commonwealth.

The London in which Henry Morgan found himself in July 1672 was already one of the great cities of Europe. Its half million inhabitants were crowded either within the confines of the City itself – bounded by its familiar gates such as Ludgate, Moorgate, Newgate, Cripplegate and Bishopsgate – or clustered into the 'Liberties' – such as Whitechapel, Stepney and Lambeth – outside the walls. Within the City there had been extensive reconstruction in the six years since the Great Fire. Much of the wattle and timber had been replaced by brick; no longer did overhanging houses almost touch each other across the streets (in the manner which had so facilitated the spread of the Fire); slender spires of Wren churches were beginning to stand up like sentinels on the skyline, although the foundation stone of the new St Paul's was not to be laid for another three years.

But while so much rebuilding had gone on, the tortuous old medieval town plan had still been largely followed. The streets remained badly cobbled and had no sidewalks; the ditches (some – like the celebrated Fleet Ditch – formidable trenches of sewage and rubble) were open; pedestrians were in more danger of street accidents caused by carriages and riders than they were of footpads. The safest and most frequented thoroughfare was the river; two thousand wherrymen plied their trade on the Thames between Tower stairs and the Privy stairs at Whitehall. But even the waterway had its dangers: the eddies and whirlpools between the massive piers of London Bridge (still the only bridge) forced the more timid passengers ashore.

Although it must have seemed a vast metropolis to Morgan, London in fact still covered a relatively small area. Charing Cross was a suburb; St James's was a new and fashionable residential area for the nobility on the western fringes of the capital; Chelsea was a rural village on the river bank; the Mile End Road itself became a country lane after Whitechapel. But London was already a sophisticated masculine shopping centre and Morgan would have been intrigued by commercial evidence of the fashionable interest in scientific discovery: the shops of the Strand and Cheapside not only sold guns and pipes, but also clocks, barometers, and musical and navigational instruments.

London must also have appeared to Morgan as a sociable city. While the taverns remained the centres of popular concourse, and doubtless the preferred haunts of Morgan, new coffee-houses were springing up where current political ideas and philosophical arguments were bandied about with ferocity. The year before Morgan's arrival these had been officially described as 'nurseries of sedition' and they were to become the object of an Act for their suppression before he left London. The ribald and frequently obscene Restoration theatre drew eager audiences: Wycherley's *Country Wife* was to have its first performance while Morgan was in London. Archery and fencing were favourite pastimes among the gentry, while cock-fighting remained the most popular spectator sport; although bear-baiting still drew some adherents, bull-baiting was considered regrettably Spanish and in bad form. Hospitality in private houses was lavish and frequent: not only the Court circle, but most of those enjoying office under the Crown kept a good table and relished entertaining their friends and patrons to large dinners in the early evening. Later in the night, the gaming-houses came into their own, where familiar dice and card games had recently been augmented by the more genteel game of *Ombre*, introduced to the country by Charles II's queen, Catherine of Braganza.

That Morgan was in trouble with the King and Council was indisputable, but there were a number of popular considerations in his favour. While it might be official policy to mend fences with Spain, public sentiment was still anti-Spanish as a facet of a deeply-felt anti-Catholicism. Morgan's arrival in London was at the beginning of a decade that was later to witness the emergence of Titus Oates and his revelations of a Popish Plot. The hysteria that followed those spurious revelations was still in the future, but there was already plenty of rabid antagonism to Popery in all its forms. Although – for instance – there was no serious evidence linking English or foreign Catholics with the start of the Great Fire of London – and indeed little reason to think that it was arson at all – the Lord Mayor deemed it appropriate to place a plaque on the site in Pudding Lane where the Fire had broken out, reading:

Here, by the permission of Heaven, Hell broke loose upon this Protestant City from the malicious hearts of barbarous papists.

English families cherished their copies of Foxe's *Book of Martyrs* with the same reverence as they attached to their English bible and their English prayer book; they shuddered over its gruesome details of the fiendish tortures inflicted by popish inquisitors. Men recalled with pride and nostalgia the days when Drake, Raleigh and other Elizabethan adventurers had singed the king of Spain's beard. Indeed, the anniversary of the accession of Queen Elizabeth was celebrated in London by burning an effigy of the Pope, with live cats sewn up in his belly 'to make him squawl realistically' (Restoration Londoners were not squeamish). Pepys himself – than whom few citizens were more loyal and industrious – was shortly to do a spell in the

Tower on account of his association with the Catholic Duke of
York. And when Nell Gwynn's carriage was surrounded by a
hostile London mob, she turned away its wrath by poking her
head out of the window and declaring 'I'm the *Protestant*
whore!' It was little wonder that Englishmen in 1672 had a soft
spot for a Protestant sea-dog who burnt Spanish papist Ba-
bylons.

They also had a soft spot for a rascal. Although it was more
than ten years since the restoration of the monarchy, many
Englishmen were still reacting against the privations of puritan-
ism: moral censure was out of fashion. A new vogue of 'popular'
literature was emerging which glorified the rogue as a hero of
romance. One almost contemporary pamphlet* comments on
this trend by saying:

> It is nothing to kill a man this week . . . to drown two
> admirals in a week, and buoy them up again the next . . .

The notorious Captain Blood had won further celebrity a few
months before Morgan's arrival by his daring attempt to steal
the crown jewels from the Tower. And a few months after his
arrival a book was published entitled *The Counterfeit Lady
Unveiled* relating the adventurous career of Mary Moders, a
lady who fired the popular imagination by such exploits as
giving herself out to be a princess, stealing the Lord Chancel-
lor's mace and appearing on the stage in a dramatization of her
own life in the intervals from prison. (However, it must be
admitted that the amused affection with which she was re-
garded did not save her from meeting her inevitable deserts on
Tyburn gallows in 1673.) Against this background the more
lurid details of Morgan's exploits did not unduly shock Londoners, while the facts of his success provided a welcome tonic
to a citizenry too long conditioned to reports of naval defeats
and humiliations.

But even more effective than this ground-swell of sympathy
were some specific allies. Chief among these was Christopher

* *The Tears of the Press* (London, 1681)

Christopher Monck, 2nd Duke of Albemarle, the Restoration rake
who was a friend and patron of Morgan

Monck, 2nd Duke of Albemarle and son of the celebrated general who had engineered the return of King Charles II to his kingdom. The Monck family were related to the Modyfords, and therefore had a family interest in the case of Sir Thomas Modyford and his associate Henry Morgan; and in addition to this link of kinship, Morgan's uncle, General Sir Thomas Morgan, had fought prominently in the Civil War alongside General Monck. Morgan thus had a double call on the young Duke's goodwill.

Apart from these links Albemarle and Morgan established an early *rapport* based on sharing a temperamental propensity for living dangerously and boisterously. Having succeeded at the age of sixteen to the dukedom and the favour of Charles II, Albemarle had been notorious – even at a Court populated by Restoration rakes – for wild and intemperate behaviour. When an officer of the law – a beadle – had attempted to force an entry to a brothel at Whetstone Park ('a scandalous place', according to a contemporary commentator) while the Dukes of Albemarle, Monmouth and Somerset were disporting themselves within, it was Albemarle who had struck him down and killed him. Not surprisingly, an infuriated mob chased the young noblemen back to Whitehall Palace where (according to one of the rhymesters around the Court):

> They need not send a messenger before
> They're too well known to stand long at the door.
> See what mishaps dare e'en invade Whitehall
> The silly fellow's death puts off the ball.

The cancellation of the court ball was the least of it; the King was furious at a scandal involving one whom he had appointed both as a Knight of the Garter and as a Gentleman of his Bedchamber. But he pardoned him for the killing none the less.

Other scandals were to follow. When a drummer in the Duke of Albemarle's regiment was charged with being drunk, his fellows mutinied at one of their number being punished for doing what 'ye officers had never been free from'. Albemarle was later to fight a duel with Lord Grey of Werke; the two principals and their seconds engaged in a four-man swordfight; when Albemarle's second was wounded and disarmed, the Duke fought on alone for a while against his two opponents until eventually surrendering his sword. Again, Charles II was furious when he heard of it.

Womanizing, drinking and duelling were coupled with other more expensive pastimes. Albemarle competed with his sovereign at the novel pastime of yachting; he kept racehorses and he gave fashionable balls at Albemarle House (on the site of the present Albemarle Street in St James's). Eventually, the day of reckoning was to come: Albemarle House had to be sold up, and his Duchess – always an eccentric lady – finally went mad.* But when Morgan arrived in London under arrest in 1672 his influential patron was still riding high.

But however much popular sentiment might be in his favour, and however influential his friends, Morgan was still in deep trouble. The Spanish faction remained determined to force the King to make an example of him; the King, for his part, had no intention of doing anything of the sort, and bided his time while allowing Morgan to marshal his defence. Morgan's justification of his actions rested essentially on two tenets: firstly, that he had not been informed of the peace treaty with Spain; and secondly, that he was acting throughout his campaign with the approbation of the Governor and Council of Jamaica.

On the former point, Modyford and Morgan confirmed each others' stories: the pinnace sent by Modyford with letters to

---

* After Albemarle's death, the Duchess – though still mad – was much courted for her wealth. She developed illusions of grandeur and declared that she would only remarry with a monarch. When Lord Montagu decided to woo her, he therefore did so disguised as the Emperor of China. His rival, Lord Roos, wrote of the incident:

> Insulting rival, never boast
>   Thy conquest lately won.
> No wonder that her heart was lost;
>   Her senses first were gone.

Morgan at Ile à Vache, telling him of the peace, had missed Morgan and the letters had been brought back to Modyford with their seals unbroken. Modyford had not known where else to send the letters. Morgan for his part had not been in touch with any other reliable source of news (one could not trust what the Spaniards said). If, as seemed all too probable, Modyford had not been overzealous in seeking out Morgan's whereabouts, and Morgan had taken good care to put to sea when the first rumours of peace reached him, these were speculations that could not be proved against either man.

On the question of Morgan's documentation, the case for the defence was even more solid. Even Sir Thomas Lynch, when sending him back under arrest, had had to concede that 'to speak the truth of him . . . he had both Sir Thomas Modyford's and the Council's commission and instruction'. And even after the full enormity of what he had done at Panama had been revealed, there was no attempt to discredit or dispute his credentials.

While Morgan mounted his defence, he did not lead the life of a recluse in Restoration London. Not only was his own temperament against such a course, the mood of London was against it too: smart society wanted to meet the controversial hero of so many bizarre exploits. He had introductions through the Albemarles and others to a number of the great houses of London, where he was lionized by the hostesses of the day. Sadly, if he ever met Samuel Pepys it was after the diary was finished and there is no record of the encounter. But John Evelyn's diary does speak of Morgan on a number of occasions: there are references to 'exploits of Coll: Morgan and others of Jamaica on the Spanish continent at Panama' and to 'business of Jamaica under our inspection on certain letters written from that Governor' coming before the Council of Plantations on which Evelyn sat; but always they seemed to be lacking a quorum and 'there was nothing done'. Eventually, however, Evelyn encountered Morgan and Modyford together on 20 October 1674 and appears to have received a racy account of the buccaneer's adventures:

Lond: Council, dined with * at my L: Berkeley's where I had
discourse with Sir Tho: Modyford, late Governor of Jamaica,
and with Coll: Morgan who undertooke that gallant exploit
from Nombre de Dios to Panama on the Continent of
America: he told me 10000 men would easily conquer all the
Spanish Indies, the[y] were so secure: greate was the booty
they tooke, and much, nay infinitely greater had it been, had
they not been betraied and so discovered before their
approach, as they had time to carry on board the vast
Treasure, which they put off to sea, in sight of our Men, that
had no boates to follow etc: They set fire to Panama, and
ravag'd the country 60 miles about.

The reference to Nombre de Dios probably reflects the fact that
ever since Drake's exploits this was the one place-name on the
Caribbean coast of the Panama isthmus known to educated
Englishmen.

Like the Council of Plantations, the King himself was in no
hurry to rush to judgment on Morgan's case: he kept him in
London, at Morgan's own very considerable expense, for well
over a year before his case was even examined. This allowed
time for Spanish resentment to simmer down. It also allowed
time for the King to consider a memorandum prepared by
Morgan (doubtless with help in the drafting) on the require-
ments for the defence of Jamaica, which was now thought to be
at risk from the Dutch. Morgan was able to convince the King
that a failure to mobilize the traditional resources of the island –
the legitimate privateers and the local militia – would put a
much heavier strain on the exchequer. The King was also
beginning to realize that Lynch had no *rapport* with these
traditional elements, whereas Morgan was their acknowledged
leader. The more familiar the King became with Morgan's
record, the more it seemed that not only were his past exploits defensible, but his qualities represented an asset for the
future.

The King presided over the final hearing of the case against
Morgan. He was cleared of all charges. Soon thereafter, in

King Charles II who knighted Morgan after his vindication in
London

January 1674, he was nominated as lieutenant governor of Jamaica. Later still, he was received in private audience by the King, dubbed a knight and told he could return home at last. Lest there should be any lingering doubts about the royal favour that shone on the new Sir Henry – and also perhaps because the steely-nerved King had taken a liking to this bold adventurer – Charles presented him with a jewelled snuff-box bearing his own portrait in miniature (a more lavish age's equivalent of the signed photograph). Few men have been more dramatically elevated from dubious notoriety to indisputable acceptance.

The King appointed Lord Vaughan to be Morgan's superior as governor. The two men got off on the wrong foot from the start: Vaughan was determined that Morgan should not reach Jamaica ahead of him and take the reins of government into his own hands. He therefore ordered the ship taking Morgan out – the *Jamaica Merchant* – to keep company with the ship on which he himself was embarked, the *Foresight*. Probably intentionally, Morgan gave the *Foresight* the slip and made a fast crossing ahead of her in the *Jamaica Merchant*. But, as so often, the seamanship at his disposal was not up to the standard of his tactical ingenuity. More likely for reasons of nostalgia rather than of navigation, the captain of the *Foresight* went close inshore at Ile à Vache (that old haunt of buccaneers where the *Oxford* had blown up under Morgan), ran aground on a coral reef and promptly sank. Morgan had been involved in the wreck of yet another ship. But this time there was no loss of life; the crew got ashore with food and water and after a few days were picked up by a passing English privateer, one Captain Rogers, who had previously sailed under Morgan. Rogers took them on to Jamaica where, despite his shipwreck, Morgan arrived a week before Lord Vaughan and was able to welcome the newcomer to 'his' island.

Charles II may have imagined that Lord Vaughan and Sir Henry Morgan would complement each other as governor and lieutenant governor. Vaughan was an effete literary figure, given to complicated and esoteric vices ('one of the lewdest fellows of the age, worse than Sir Charles Sedley', according to Pepys, whose descriptions of Sedley's capers have been decreed 'too gross for printing' in all but the most definitive editions of the diaries); while Morgan was synonymous with all that was robust and coarse-grained, essentially a man of action. But far from constituting a satisfactory team of contrasting talents, the governor and lieutenant governor fell out: Vaughan was soon complaining to London that 'Sir Henry had made himself and his authority cheap' by drinking in vulgar taverns with common seamen; while Morgan and his friends, for their part, were complaining to London that Vaughan did nothing to stop Spanish harassment of the English logwood cutters on the Mosquito coast.

The action which finally damaged Vaughan's reputation beyond repair with the Jamaicans was his treatment of a dubious privateer called Captain Browne. Vaughan had Browne arrested for piracy and rushed through his execution without allowing time for the island assembly to consider petitions in his favour. This was bad enough, but what really worried the islanders was that they thought Browne's summary hanging would scare away all those other privateers on whose activities the defence of Jamaica had for so long depended. By 1678, with war – this time with France – looming, the Privy Council in London had accepted the view, long held by the islanders, that Vaughan was not the man to protect Jamaica. He was recalled, but there was no hurry to send out a successor, and Morgan was left in charge as lieutenant governor.

Morgan wasted no time in setting in order the defences of Port Royal: the old forts were repaired and new ones built. Few people knew better than he how to look for weaknesses in fortifications, and his work immeasurably strengthened the port. It was not only land defences which were indicated: the French might be expected to intercept merchant ships carrying home the produce of Jamaica. Morgan organized convoys of ships, with armed escort vessels, for the voyages to London and Bristol. In the event, none of his precautions was put to the test: the French admiral, Count d'Estrées, and his fleet destroyed

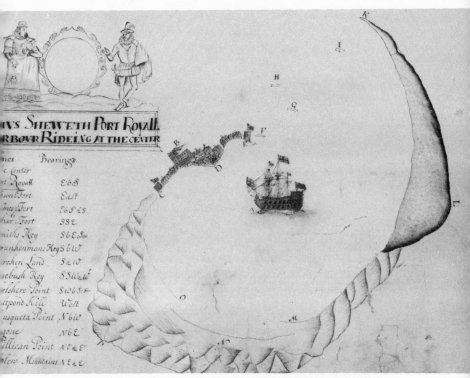

A map of Port Royal harbour attributed to William Hack, who redrew maps sent by Morgan for the Duke of Albemarle. This one was probably drawn in the 1680s, despite the earlier costume of the figures, and comes from the collection of Sir Hans Sloane

themselves by running on to Caribbean coral reefs in the middle of the night of 4 May 1678. Thirteen ships were wrecked and five hundred lives lost. (Morgan may have felt some fellow-feeling for d'Estrées after his own loss of *Satisfaction* and three other ships on a reef off the mouth of the Chagres.) Jamaica basked in its new-found security and Morgan enjoyed some months of governing the island and consolidating his plantations.

In due course, another new governor arrived in the person of the Earl of Carlisle. Though, like Vaughan, an imperious aristocrat in many ways, Carlisle was both more experienced –

he had fought in the Civil War as a young man and been ambassador to Russia in later life – and more tactful; he set up his own headquarters in Spanish Town and allowed Morgan to remain cock of the roost in Port Royal. He also gave Morgan a free hand to continue the fortifying of Jamaica in the face of renewed French threats: there was a further alarm in July 1679 when Count d'Estrées returned to Jamaican waters.

Among the most important tasks which Carlisle laid on Morgan was the preparation of a report for the Privy Council in London recommending that it should in future be made a crime for a privateer to serve under a foreign flag against a country at peace with England. This cut the ground from under the feet of those quasi-privateers who had, in fact, been pirates operating under licences issued by third countries. Morgan had always been punctilious himself, in his active days, about operating with a valid privateer's commission issued by the governor of Jamaica; now he was equally demanding towards others. Either buccaneers were licensed and encouraged by him as an auxiliary arm of national defence, or they were unlicensed (or improperly licensed by foreign authorities) and treated as pirates to be hunted down and condemned to be hanged when caught.

In his pursuit of pirates, Morgan was careful not to deter those legitimate privateers on whose irregular activities so much of Jamaica's security still depended. When Carlisle left for England, taking Morgan's report to the Privy Council with him, Morgan found himself in charge for another year. During this period he captured a Dutch pirate called Evertsen together with his sloop and crew of seventy. True to his principles, he saw that they were duly sentenced to death; but, true to his prudent instincts, he saw that they were not executed lest their deaths should frighten more genuine privateers away from Jamaica at a time when he was offering an amnesty. Lord Vaughan would have done well to have adopted a policy similarly compounded of justice tempered with public interest.

But however consistent Morgan might have been in his attitude towards pirates on the one hand and privateers on the other, there were always those who resented this poacher

turned gamekeeper. Stories of his duplicity were always circu-
lating in the West Indies and reaching London. He was alleged
to have invited a whole ship's company of inadequately-licensed
privateers to dine with him as guests at King's House, to have
plied them with wine and spirits till their prudence and discretion had evaporated, to have encouraged them to confess to
illegal exploits and piratical plans and then – when they had
implicated themselves beyond recovery – to have had them
arrested, tried and hanged. The tale seems unlikely. Morgan
had no great interest in 'decorating Gallows Point' (as contem-
poraries called the process) and indeed was on more than one
occasion criticized by London for being too reluctant to shed
blood – a criticism which must have raised a wry smile on other
lips as well as his own. In general, however, the Privy Council
were well pleased with the manner in which he ensured the
security of Jamaica without incurring expense to the exchequer.

But even Morgan's vigilance on the King's behalf in Jamaica
could not protect him from those in London – including
Vaughan and Lynch – dedicated to working against him. An
admiralty court case, over which Morgan had presided in
Jamaica, involving the smuggling of brandy into the colony and
the subsequent impounding of a ship, had been made the
subject of an appeal to the Lords of Trade in London. Now,
under the influence of Morgan's old antagonists, they found
against him. Worse still, the King was persuaded to grant a
commission to Sir Thomas Lynch replacing Morgan as lieutenant governor. Not long after Lynch's return to the island, he
managed to implicate Morgan with riots in Port Royal and have
him removed from the Council and from his other public
offices. He even managed to produce a witness to swear that
Morgan had said 'God damn the Assembly', and that there had
been other 'extravagant expressions of Sir Henry in his wine'.

Indeed, now that he was removed from office, Morgan spent
more and more of his time 'in his wine'. He retired from Port
Royal to his estates at Llanrhymney (named after his birthplace) and entertained his old shipmates and a variety of
dubious seafaring acquaintances. His forays into Port Royal,

now that he no longer had councils to attend, were to wharfside
taverns and notorious stews. His loss of his seat on the Council
rankled with him, as did the libels on his honour and military
reputation contained in Esquemeling's accounts of his exploits,
now published for the first time in English and in London.
Morgan instituted lawsuits against the printers: he maintained
vigorously and successfully that he had never been a pirate, that
he had not come to Jamaica as an indentured servant but as a
soldier of fortune, that he had not 'pistolled' nuns, that he had
not blown up prisoners at Portobello, that he had not swindled
his shipmates . . . in fact, that he had behaved like an officer
and a gentleman throughout.

Then finally, in the evening of his days, his fortunes changed
for the better again. Not only did he receive damages for the
libels that had been written about him, but – better news still –
his old friend and benefactor Christopher Monck, 2nd Duke of
Albemarle, was appointed Governor of Jamaica. Albemarle
looked on the post as a means to shore up his shattered fortunes.
But he arrived at Port Royal in December 1687 already a very
sick man: although only aged thirty-four, he was suffering
severely from the effects of his overindulgence at the Restoration court. Indeed, the most prominent member of his suite was
his physician – Dr Sloane, later, as Sir Hans Sloane, to become
celebrated for his writings about West Indian flora and fauna,
for his presidency of the Royal Society, for his founding bequest
to the British Museum and, perhaps above all, for his purchase
of the Manor of Chelsea which led to the giving of his name to
Sloane Square and Sloane Street in London.

It did not take Albemarle long to set in train Morgan's
reinstatement to the Council and to restore him to the high
prestige he had formerly enjoyed on the island. But it was not
honours and position that were Morgan's real requirement
now: it was health. Dr Sloane was even more worried about
Morgan than about Albemarle. He noted that the old buccaneer
(he was probably fifty-three) could not stand without his legs
swelling up, and that – despite his paunch – he had little
appetite for food, though much for rum. He diagnosed the

'dropsie'. Morgan grew impatient with cures that involved rest and less drinking, and gave up Sloane's advice.

Morgan had lived hard, and fifty-three was a good age in the seventeenth century. It came as a surprise to few when on 25 August 1688 the old swashbuckler finally collapsed and died. His body was brought in from his plantations to lie at King's House in Port Royal. A brief amnesty allowed those of his former privateering companions who had turned to piracy to attend the funeral with impunity. The Duke led the mourners. The guns of the forts he had built fired a governor's salute. The taverns were stilled. The Caribbean would never be such a lively or dangerous place again.

10

Jamaica: Morgan's own Island

When Caroline and I sailed into Kingston harbour, just under three hundred years later, we were greeted by much which Morgan would have found familiar. The channel into the vast, almost landlocked anchorage still kept its careful course between the treacherous South, Lime and other cays; on the starboard bow Fort Charles – almost at the point of the Port Royal peninsula – still kept its commanding view over the channel; on the port bow Gallows Point still served as a reminder of the price of overstepping the mark between privateering and piracy. Also on the port side, Fort Augusta, though it would have looked of recognizable construction to Morgan, would not in fact have been familiar to him, as it was only erected some fifty years after his death. But the big surprise would have been the sprawling metropolis of Kingston itself, facing Port Royal across the harbour. It was here, in the city which had replaced both Port Royal and Spanish Town as the capital of the island, that our quest for Henry Morgan's Jamaica had necessarily to start.

Our first night ashore, at a cocktail party at the High Commissioner's residence, Trafalgar House, we encountered an unexpected ally. Miss Maud Fyfe-Fawcett had lived for more than half her fifty-odd years in Jamaica, her father – we gathered – having been a senior official in the colony's legal service. But she had found that life in Jamaica had not kept up with her expectations of it. Independence from Britain, the cessation of Government House garden parties, the growth of violence, rising prices, package tourism . . . all these were almost equally regrettable developments in her view. However, she had decided to sit it out and, having so decided, to put a brave face on it: not for her the grumbles of the disillusioned tax-dodgers or the sun-worshipping expatriates. Nor had tropical climes induced in her any propensity to compromise with local standards of dress or behaviour, and her vocabulary still owed more to Roedean and the Pytchley than to the residential quarter of Kingston where she lived. She heard of our interest in Morgan with enthusiasm.

'Harry Morgan got up to a good deal of yo-ho-ho around this neck of the woods, y'know. I'll run you down to Port Royal tomorrow and we'll have a sniff around some of his old lairs if you like.'

Miss Fyfe-Fawcett arrived to collect us from Trafalgar House at 9 a.m., wearing a long flowered dress and flat sensible shoes. Caroline climbed into the front seat of her elderly Rover, while she cleared room for me on the back seat by tossing out of the way a tennis racket, whose two broken strings suggested that it was more a symbol of a way of life than an active instrument of pleasure.

We swung out of the High Commission compound on to a busy road heading to the eastern end of Kingston harbour, passing through Harbour View, and then turning sharply to the west along a narrow spit of stony land which forms the southern boundary of Kingston harbour. We passed the Norman Manley Airport, the lighthouse and the yacht club, and continued westwards towards the point of the peninsula on which stands Port Royal. The first indication we had of approaching buccaneer haunts was a large archway marked 'Morgan's Harbour' on our right.

'Nothing to see there except a few tarted-up boats on a tarted-up beach,' said our driver, putting her foot down both metaphorically and literally.

The main feature of Port Royal is Fort Charles, built in Morgan's lifetime, largely under his direction. In the seventeenth century the sea came right up to the massive stone walls of Fort Charles, as is witnessed by the iron mooring rings secured in the masonry. Not only was the fort named after King Charles II, but a considerable proportion of that monarch's share of the proceeds of the buccaneers' expeditions was devoted to improving the armament and fortifications of the place.

We walked around the walls. On the southern, seaward side we could see the gun-pits dug in the nineteenth century to protect the harbour against potential invaders even more formidable than the Spaniards. Indeed, the decline of Port Royal in the eighteenth century in no way diminished the strategic significance of the Fort Charles promontory, because as the commercial importance of Port Royal diminished so that of Kingston grew, and the promontory overlooking the only entrance to its harbour remained relevant to defence. As a further reminder of the continued importance of the fort, a plaque commemorates the sojourn of Lord Nelson here. He – like Morgan – had patrolled these walls.

Few wicked cities have met with more instant retribution than Port Royal. Four years after Morgan's death it was subjected to a ferocious earthquake: fissures opened up in the ground; all but the stoutest buildings collapsed; ships were washed by tidal waves into the centre of the town. But the earthquake which destroyed Port Royal in 1692 was not the last to shake the promontory. Just outside the walls we saw a solid brick building, which might well have been an ammunition shed for the gun emplacements, but which was tilted at a curious angle and is now known as the Giddy House.

We walked through the half-empty little streets of Port Royal. First our guide took us to a large, long, barrack-like building on the northern shore of the peninsula. This had been built as a British military hospital in 1819 with iron girders brought by sea from England. The whole edifice had a Meccano-like look which belied its durability. Now it housed the museum of Port Royal and the centre of archaeological research. We walked through well laid-out rooms of trophies, photographs, models and maps; Sir Henry Morgan would, we felt, have been gratified to see this memorial to the town he loved, but he might have missed seeing evidence of those taverns and gaming-houses where Lord Vaughan had so censoriously reported that he had made himself cheap.

The defences of Fort Charles, in which Morgan interested himself, at
Port Royal in Jamaica

Miss Fyfe-Fawcett too was worried that we had not got
sufficient feeling for – as she put it – the yo-ho-ho side of Harry
Morgan. She kept stopping to tell us that every stone on which
we walked was probably the doorstep of a gambling hell or the
lintel of a house of ill repute.

'Randy lot, those buccaneers,' she said, and I thought she
was going to go on to say they would have been less so if they had
played more organized games or taken up field sports.

'Mind you,' she added, 'the dagos were just as bad. Did you
know,' she lowered her voice, 'there was a whole boatload of
tarts attached to the Spanish Armada? Never kept up with the
fleet. Ran aground in France. And you can imagine what *that*
must have led to!'

We imagined.

One curious monument in Port Royal would certainly have appealed to the survival instincts of Morgan. In the church is the tomb of a Huguenot contemporary of his who was buried twice. This worthy merchant had the misfortune to be swallowed up in a rift of the earth which opened up on the shore of Port Royal during that earthquake of 1692 which was viewed by many as clear evidence of God's judgement on the wicked town. Perhaps the Huguenot had been less sinful than the rest, or perhaps he was just more lucky, because according to contemporary accounts 'he was spewed out alive from the earth' and found himself floating safely off shore – just as Morgan had found himself after the explosion on the frigate *Oxford*. The good merchant appeared to have been none the worse for his adventure, and it was many years after his rescue that he found his final resting-place at the church.

Morgan's remains were less lucky. He had been buried in the stony graveyard half way along the road between Port Royal and the mainland. The earthquake shattered this section of the promontory, and no stone remains to mark the resting-place of the greatest of the buccaneers.

Morgan's friend and patron, Sir Thomas Modyford, had found a safer and more durable resting-place. He is buried under the Cathedral Church of St Jago de la Vega, now known as Spanish Town. The cathedral, built on the site of an earlier Spanish church, has been altered, extended and restored many times, usually following the ravages of hurricanes. During one of the 'improvements', in 1848, Modyford's own vault was excavated, despite the fact that it was fifteen feet below the level of the cathedral pavement; it was found to contain 'much gold lace', as befitted a Stuart grandee. Modyford's connection with the cathedral was strong even in his lifetime, because at that period the Assembly of the island met at the cathedral, and it was to Spanish Town that Morgan hastened to make his reports in person to the governor on return from his exploits.

It was hither, in Miss Fyfe-Fawcett's Rover, that we too hastened to make our next excursion. Today Spanish Town is an eighteenth-century rather than a seventeenth-century town.

The old colonial square in Spanish Town, Jamaica, with Admiral
Rodney's memorial on the left

Its handsome square with lawns and palm trees, flanked on its
four sides by the King's House, the House of Assembly, the
Courts of Law, and a striking memorial to Admiral Lord
Rodney, remind the visitor of the civil and ordered world of the
Augustans rather than the fortified chaos of the buccaneers'
Port Royal.

Miss Fyfe-Fawcett lingered in front of the Rodney memorial.
She pondered reverently over the figure of Britannia, portrayed
as being drawn by dolphins through the wreckage of the French
fleet after the Battle of the Saints. She gazed with awe at the
emblazoned coronets and heraldic devices of Lord Rodney's
coat of arms. She eyed with approval the statue of the admiral
himself – his haughty, elegant figure set off by the Roman toga
in which the sculptor had chosen to portray him.

'Now there's a man it really *would* be worth writing about,' she said. 'Every inch an officer and a gentleman. I'm sure I read somewhere,' she went on, 'that Lord Rodney always used to change his cravat and shave before going into battle . . . said he wanted to face his Maker looking as he would like to appear before their Lordships of the Admiralty. Not, of course, that your Captain Morgan wasn't very sporting in his way, but one feels he might have been a bit of an embarrassment in the wardroom; and one fears he might have been a bit forgetful about changing his cravat and that sort of thing.'

I thought of Morgan on the Las Cruces trail, in the stews of Port Royal or torturing the prisoners at Portobello.

'You could be right,' I said. 'Perhaps he wasn't very good at that sort of thing.' (Privately I wondered whether that hard-gambling and notoriously philandering Admiral Rodney was himself really such a model of Dartmouth values as Miss Fyfe-Fawcett appeared to believe.)

Just off the square is the office of the Jamaican archives. We were shown round by Mr Clinton Black, for many years the government archivist in Jamaica. One of his most treasured possessions is Sir Henry Morgan's will. This left everything to his wife, apart from a few personal gifts, such as a green saddle to one friend and the choice of any one of his horses and his 'blew saddle and furniture thereunto belonging together with one case of pistolls tipped with silver' to another. He also left a number of mourning rings, including one to his friend and supporter the Duke of Albemarle. After his wife's death his property was to pass to his nephews on condition that they adopted the surname of the childless buccaneer. Mr Clinton Black can trace his own professional line of descent direct from that island secretary who was granted a commission to keep the records in 1659 and whose office recorded Morgan's own property purchase.

For in the last part of his life Morgan showed an increasing taste for the role of planter and squire. The seadog had come into harbour; the governor had fallen from public office; the reveller now sometimes – under the ever more pressing admonitions of his doctor – took himself away from the fleshpots of Port

Royal to the quieter recreations of his estates inland or on the north coast. It was time we pursued his traces there too.

We bade a grateful farewell to Miss Fyfe-Fawcett.

'Don't fancy the north coast much m'self,' she said. 'Too many smart people wearing too few clothes: sort of Royal Enclosure in bikinis. At least, that's what it *was* like. Got a bit tatty now. And as for the goings-on at that place Negril! That's just Epsom Heath in the altogether: starkers little numbers wandering around bold as buttons. Not my scene. Might have been Harry Morgan's, mind you. Anyhow. . . .'

Her final well-wishes were lost in the splutter of the Rover's departure.

Our drive around the east end of the island, skirting the Blue Mountains, was through country with less direct connection with Morgan than those places we had so far visited. But during Morgan's time as governor Port Morant and the other little bays and harbours we passed had often sheltered those buccaneers who had not dared to put in to Port Royal until they had made discreet enquiries about what their reception was likely to be. Sometimes they were misled into a false sense of security, like those who were reported to have dined with Morgan and

Admiral Rodney's coat of arms on the Spanish Town memorial

boasted of their past and projected acts of piracy. Sometimes they put to sea again before the harsh régime of later days could catch up with them.

Our first port of call on the north coast was to be Llanrhymney, the estate which Morgan had bought and named after his birthplace in Wales. Little but the name remains to perpetuate the connection, although a few miles further west we were told we could see a building which had once been a part of Morgan's establishment here and was now known as Morgan's kitchen. It was on the property of the late Sir Noel Coward, and it was towards this great minstrel's hideaway that we now climbed up from the coast.

We had expected that the Coward villa – still preserved as the master had left it – would be a haven of luxury, redolent of Las Vegas, tuxedos, and silken dressing-gowns. The reality was surprisingly austere: a tiny house in which access to each room seemed to involve going through all the others, and a swimming pool of diminutive proportions and starkly rectangular shape. Only the view was remarkable: this encompassed a great sweep of coastline stretching out towards the cays of Cuba. There were two constructions on the broad grass sward between the villa and the view. One was a solid stone edifice partly concealed by bougainvillaea: this was the alleged kitchen of Morgan's house. Perhaps the foundations had indeed been those of the kitchen; perhaps not; nothing external suggested any connection with the seventeenth century. The other construction appeared to be a high railing enclosing a few square yards of ground. We sauntered over to it and found ourselves looking at the tombstone of Noel Coward: an Englishman laid to rest under the midday sun of those tropical climes which he had immortalized in cheerful jingle for so many of his compatriots.

It would have been hard to think of any two Englishmen so contrasting in their life-styles as those two elderly knights – Sir Noel Coward and Sir Henry Morgan. But only a few miles further up the coast had lived a compatriot who had created a character much closer to the spirit of the old buccaneer. Ian Fleming had devised the adventures of that latter-day swashbuckler James Bond at his villa Goldeneye on the outskirts of Port Maria. We were taken there by Blanche Blackwell, an old friend of his, who had restored Goldeneye to how it had been in Fleming's lifetime: the Jamaican hardwood desk on which he wrote the novels, the original print of the Goldeneye duck after which the house was named, the room where Sir Anthony Eden had stayed after his health and the Suez campaign had collapsed almost simultaneously, the posters for the James Bond films on the walls . . . all these were as they had been. Again, there was an unexpected frugality about the bare rooms, and for the genuine sybaritic flavour of James Bond's world we had to go to Blanche's own exquisite villa on higher ground nearby.

Sipping our rum punches before lunch we became intrigued by the sumptuous pile of books on tropical fish and coral reefs lying on the terrace table. We soon discovered we were in the presence of an expert. Blanche could describe to us the difference between squirrelfish and goatfish, between cherubfish and angelfish, or between staghorn and elkhorn coral. Noting our interest, she fitted us up with masks, snorkel tubes and flippers, and took us out to the reefs off Goldeneye. Here Ian Fleming had developed that passion for underwater pursuits that was to feature in so many of James Bond's adventures. The toothy, protruding lower jaw of a four-foot barracuda gliding menacingly between the fire coral gave us a sharp reminder of the perils of these waters. Henry Morgan was haunted by such coral reefs as that over which we were swimming. His ships frequently damaged themselves on uncharted reefs along the Main and off the islands and cays of the Caribbean, and twice – as we have seen – he had had a ship sunk under him on a reef such as this.

From Port Maria we continued westwards along the north coast of the island. We had now seen almost everywhere directly connected with Captain Morgan in Jamaica, but we wanted to get some idea of what Morgan's last years in retirement on his estates must have been like. Life at Laurencefield, the plantation house once associated with Morgan on the south side of the island, no longer revealed the pattern of life of the early plantation years. But one of the great houses of Jamaica where

Good Hope, one of the 'great houses' of colonial times in Jamaica,
where the author received assistance on his travels

life is still lived at this tempo is Good Hope, near Falmouth.
There we had been invited to spend a few days with Patrick
Tenison and his family.

Good Hope was not built until more than sixty years after
Henry Morgan had been laid in his all-too-briefly-frequented
grave. But the house has as much the feeling of the seventeenth
as of the eighteenth century: a high porticoed front, polished
hardwood floors, tall ceilings allowing the circulation of air,
stone-built stables, and terraced lawns looking out over broad
acres of cattle ranch, coconut groves and sugar plantations. In
the evenings we would ride with Patrick round the estate.

Morgan would have recognized the layout of the former slave
lines and approved of the remains of the solid stone slave
hospital. He would have seen no change in the manner in which
an ancient black man split the husks off the coconuts: a good
worker then as now could shell sixteen hundred a day. He

would have been surprised to see the prevalence of miniature palms replacing the older, taller trees, and he might have been startled by the huge white brahmin cattle, with their long horns, as these were only introduced to Jamaica by the British in 1860 from India (on the sensible assumption that such hardy beasts would do equally well in other hot climates). He might well have been even more startled by a small animal which ran out of the undergrowth beneath our horses' hooves and which he could never have seen: a mongoose, also introduced from India, but not so much to kill snakes as to keep down the rats.

But the leisurely pace of life, the cool rum drinks on the cool wide verandah of the Great House, the chanting of the Africans in the fields, the chatter of a parrot brought back from a foraging trip to the Main . . . these sights and sounds and sensations would have solaced Henry Morgan as he passed his last years on his estates, just as they solaced us. It was easy to imagine at Good Hope that all had always been peaceful there, but this was not so.

Only a few miles behind the estate, in the mountainous terrain to the south, lies the notorious cockpit country. This is a region of forested ravines, inhabited for several centuries by the Maroons – a fierce tribe of freed slaves of African extraction – who had been a factor affecting the tranquillity of the island since the time of Morgan.

Indeed, it was when the English under Penn and Venables first invaded and occupied Jamaica that the Spanish colonial authorities had freed and armed their slaves, leaving them behind in these mountains to form an irregular guerrilla force – in support of their own more conventional stay-behind party under Don Cristobal Arnoldo – to harass the new English settlers. From these early days the Maroons had indulged in periodical raids into the settled areas to burn the sugar cane, rob the planters' houses and occasionally slaughter – in gruesome fashion – the planters themselves. Their hideaways in the cockpit country provided a refuge for runaway slaves from all over the colony and their numbers grew menacingly large.

Although it was not until forty-five years after Morgan's

death that the Maroon problem reached such proportions that the government had to build a chain of forts around the edge of the cockpit country and launch a full-scale military campaign against them, none the less the Maroons were a recurring nuisance and an intermittent threat in Morgan's lifetime.

Over a rum daiquiri on the verandah of Good Hope, one of Patrick's guests – a planter whose family had been on the island for many generations – told us that there was a local tradition that after one particularly bloody Maroon raid in the 1680s the community around Falmouth had decided that a punitive counter-raid must be made into the cockpit country to seek out and destroy the Maroon strongholds. Only one man on the island had the experience of irregular jungle warfare to qualify him to lead such an expedition: the man who had led a prolonged approach march through the swamps around Villahermosa, who had braved the forest ambuscades between the Bay of Santa Maria and Puerto Principe, who had survived Indian arrows in the gullies of the isthmus of Panama. The superannuated lieutenant governor was approached.

Henry Morgan was not attracted by the prospect of such an active assignment in his later forties. He had put on much weight and grown accustomed to the sedentary life of a seventeenth-century planter. Exertion tired him now. He had lost touch with the rank and file of the buccaneers who were the only troops he knew how to lead. Besides, Morgan must have realized that the success of his exploits had been due in no small measure to the fact that his men were more adept at living in rough conditions than were the Spaniards against whom they were fighting. This advantage would not apply in any campaign against the Maroons, who would enjoy complete mastery of their environment in the mountainous defiles and thickets, while Morgan and whatever force he had been able to scrape together would be the interlopers operating at a disadvantage. Defending Port Royal was one thing; going out to look for trouble in the cockpit country quite another.

According to the local tradition, my informant continued, Morgan had agreed to conduct a reconnaissance – not to locate

Another aspect of Good Hope: such mellowed plantation buildings
were the scene of Morgan's last years

and engage the Maroons, but to gauge the nature of the terrain
and advise the authorities on how they should mount an
expedition. It is not known what advice he gave, but it is known
that a few years later the authorities imported Indians from the
Mosquito coast of Nicaragua in a vain attempt to hunt and put
down the Maroons; later still, towards the end of the eighteenth
century, the Jamaican government introduced man-hunting
mastiffs which succeeded in putting terror into the hearts of the
Maroons in a way which neither columns of redcoats nor bands
of Mosquito Indians had managed to do. At all events, it seems
likely that Morgan did not unduly exert or hazard himself by his
reconnoitring, since no record of it reached the official archives,
which are explicit enough about most of his activities right up to
the time of his death.

'If you're wanting to have some last excitements in retracing
Captain Morgan's exploits, you ought to do as he did – a quick

dip into the cockpit country as a final fling,' said our host. 'We might even manage to find you a Maroon guide.'

When Patrick Leigh Fermor had visited Jamaica in the 1940s he seemed to have had little difficulty in encountering an adept and delightful Maroon escort, but to have experienced considerable difficulty and danger in encountering any Rastafarians. More than thirty years later, we had the opposite experience: everywhere in Jamaica we came across 'Rastas' – bearded, Ethiopia-orientated, reggae-singing eccentrics; but we tried in vain to locate a Maroon guide who could escort us to the cockpit country.

Eventually, one of the coconut splitters at Good Hope said he had a brother-in-law who had a cousin who had a friend who knew a Maroon who knew the cockpit country. Surprisingly, this tenuous chain of acquaintance resulted in the materialization of a dark, wizened gentleman called Obadiah, with whom Caroline and I some days later descended from a Range Rover between the villages of Flagstaff and Horse Guards and set off to penetrate the western side of the region. (The place names of this part of Jamaica perpetuate the impression of being involved in a permanent confrontation between redcoats and Maroons: a few miles further east, Windsor and Balaclava are found facing 'Me no sen, you no come' and 'Look Behind'.)

Obadiah set off at a brisk gait which had a disconcerting resemblance to the dreaded 'scout's pace' of my boyhood: a hundred yards of running alternating with a hundred yards of walking. We had been prepared for this by recollections of Leigh Fermor's companion who, although in his late seventies, was to be seen:

> running and leaping barefoot downhill, negotiating the rocks with an agility that left us plodding far behind.*

We too also soon gave up any pretence of accompanying Obadiah's jogging bouts, and – much disappointed in us – he settled down to a more sedate pace.

* *The Traveller's Tree* (London, 1950)

What makes the cockpit country distinctive, if not unique, among mountainous, tropical woodlands is the prevalence of precipices. A thousand miles to the south-east, among the upper tributaries of the Orinoco in Venezuela, there is a region of small, high plateaux of forest each surrounded by steep cliffs which convert them into inaccessible table-lands – into, in fact, the model for Conan Doyle's *The Lost World*. Here in the cockpit country the process is reversed: there are a series of low-lying saucers of land surrounded by high precipices. The intruders, instead of being stranded on top like the heroes of Conan Doyle's story, are hemmed in below and frequently unable to find any route to climb out of the 'cockpit'. This was how government troops had been trapped and shot down on their punitive expedition against the Maroons, and this was how we found ourselves totally dependent upon Obadiah to make any progress through this beautiful but menacing terrain, in which – again to quote Leigh Fermor's words –

all is hostile and withdrawn and the meridian demon that is the genius of the place blinds the air and the rocks and the forest in a conspiracy to send the intruder to Coventry.

It would surely have reminded Morgan of the worst gullies encountered on the Las Cruces trail, and he would doubtless have calculated that the liberated Maroons would be more formidable than the Indian vassals of the Spaniards. Even if he had – at the time – been a long way off becoming the dropsical figure with the swollen legs described by Dr Sloane, he must still have found it difficult to hoist his paunch over the crags and through the narrow defiles. One suspects that the reconnaissance was a fairly short one, and that his refusal to lead a substantive expedition of such an uncomfortable and unprofitable nature was a fairly robust one.

In the days of the Maroon wars, the narrow defiles between the rocks had enabled the mountain dwellers to withdraw from one 'cockpit' to another, while their pursuers sought in vain to find the way to follow them. Obadiah led us through one such labyrinth of gullies and eventually, when we had caught up with him, turned to us and said:

'Now you want to see something naughty?'

It was a curiously unexpected and out-of-context remark. Had he brought us all this way to show us dirty postcards? Surely not: he looked a most respectable elder citizen. Were there Maroon girls cavorting in the rock pools? It hardly seemed likely in the sepulchral hush of the oppressive forest. Perhaps the word 'naughty' had some special local connotation: did it mean a risky path along a rock ledge?

While we were still puzzling, he dived ahead of us through a thicket between two boulders; we followed on his heels so as not to lose sight of him and emerged on to a shelf of open cultivated land, perhaps a quarter of an acre in size. The crop eluded recognition.

'Very naughty, very naughty!' said Obadiah, wagging a finger at the stiff, tall green plants that covered the carefully tilled soil.

'What is it? Why is it naughty?' we echoed in unison.

Obadiah mimed smoking a cigarette with his right hand while he made a gesture of screwing the forefinger of his left hand into the side of his head:

'You go good trip on this stuff, man.'

We were looking at a field of marijuana.

'This not grown by Maroons. This grown by bad men from Montego Bay. They use Maroons to bring them here where police no see. They don't like nosy-parking.'

It seemed to me that place names like 'Me no sen, you no come' had not altogether lost their relevance in these parts.

'Ganja crop make much money. Bad men very rich. All come here with guns. If they find us here – "Poof! Poof!"' Obadiah made a realistic shooting-from-the-hip gesture.

'Then perhaps we should not hang around,' I suggested, not wanting to be accused of nosy-parking.

Obadiah did not go back on his tracks. Instead, he skirted the marijuana field and disappeared up another cleft in the rocks. Soon we had lost all sense of direction. Vistas opened up over yet further 'cockpits'; precipices materialized at our feet; water-falls cascaded above us; a brilliantly coloured serpent rustled off through the leaves ahead of us; this was the Garden of Eden as Cranach might have seen it – but after the Fall: a spirit of malevolence was abroad.

Suddenly we lost Obadiah altogether: one moment he was there, the next he was not. He could not have gone to the left; there was a sharp precipice falling away on that side. Ahead, the path was open and there was no sign of him. To the right, there was a cliff wall rising above us. While we stood, gyrating in confusion on the path, a dark arm emerged from the greenery covering the cliff face on the right and grabbed me: Obadiah was pulling us after him into a cave the entrance of which was totally concealed by creepers. We followed, unresisting, into a dark, dank interior, and when our eyes had adjusted to the lack of light we could see that Obadiah – a finger raised to his lips – was motioning us to silence.

Then we heard the soft tread of rubber soles on the path we had just left, and the murmur of conversation. Someone – or rather several people – were coming down the jungle path from the opposite direction. They would pass directly in front of our retreat in the cave, only a few feet, in fact, from where we huddled, silent and apprehensive. These could only be Oba-diah's 'bad men'. Caroline and I consoled ourselves with the thought that, since we had not been able to see Obadiah, the mouth of the cave must be invisible from the path.

Certainly the reverse was not true: we could see through the foliage everything that passed on the track. And it was not long before we had something to see. A single file of five men, all in khaki slacks and shirts, their black faces pouring sweat, were advancing at a crisp pace. Nor was there any ambiguity about the leather pouches strapped to their belts: these men were armed with pistols. At any moment, I thought with mounting alarm, the 'Poof! Poof!' would begin.

One of the men was sweating more than the others for the good reason that he was carrying a heavier load. Almost im-mediately outside the entrance to our cave, he let out a grunt of exhaustion and swung his pack down from his shoulders and on to the path.

'This place'll do as well as any other. Not too much cover overhead, and we must be getting near the spot anyway.' He started unstrapping his pack and extending an aerial from what was clearly a portable radio transmitter.

'Calling Charlie Baker Two. Calling Charlie Baker Two. Can you hear me? Can you hear me? Angel Seven here.'

The five men squatted round the instrument on the path. Eventually, after two or three minutes, it seemed they were getting some response from Charlie Baker Two – whoever or whatever that might be.

We had not long to await the identity of their radio interlocutor: a small monoplane circling the treetops came first into earshot and then into view. The radio operator was obviously receiving now; he made notes, and kept looking up as if for landmarks among the rock-strewn scenery. The aircraft dipped low, so low it disappeared from view among the trees in the direction from which we had come. It must, I thought, be right over the marijuana field now.

Then the penny dropped. It was a spotter plane, radioing directions to the men in front of us, and giving visible indications of how they could find the illicit crop. At the same moment the significance of the matching khaki trousers and shirts, the identical pistol holsters and the uniform rubber-soled shoes struck me. These were policemen. We were in the company of the law and not at the mercy of Obadiah's bad men from Montego Bay.

I pulled Obadiah as far back as I could into the recesses of the cave and whispered to him my conviction that we had nothing to fear. We had surely encountered a patrol sent out to find and destroy a marijuana field already located from the air. Should we not reveal ourselves and offer our services?

Obadiah's response could hardly have been more negative had I suggested jumping over the precipice in front of us. He blanched, shook his head and repeated his gestures urging silence. Reluctantly Caroline and I resumed our vigil; we were on Obadiah's home ground and we felt it would be not only discourteous but wrong to overrule his clear disinclination to emerge from the cave while the police patrol was outside. Perhaps his caution was prudent: it is not always easy to explain to foreign constabularies why one is deep in an inaccessible forest near to the scene of a crime. At all events, the patrol soon moved on in the direction of the marijuana field, and – giving them good time to get well out of sight – we moved smartly in the opposite direction.

When we were sure we were safely out of earshot of the patrol, I questioned Obadiah about his reactions.

'Man, I told you those bad men who get rich by selling ganja crop use simple Maroon folk as guides in the cockpit country. I tell you right. They use me!'

Obadiah told us the whole story of his involvement in the illicit ganja trade, of the way he had been bullied into recruitment and blackmailed into continued service. If he had been found by the police near a ganja field they would have (rightly) assumed he was guilty of involvement; and if he had been reported as seen with a police patrol in the forest, the drug traffickers would have (wrongly) assumed that he had betrayed them. In the former case he would have spent a spell in prison; in the latter case, he would have ended up in small pieces on the rubbish dump outside his village.

Our return journey was less light-hearted than our outward one had been. Now we were accessories after a crime, malefactors in this Garden of Eden: every rustle in the undergrowth held the menace of an ambush, and Obadiah's galloping gait seemed to have the urgency of a fugitive's flight.

Captain Morgan had left the cockpit country, according to the legend at Good Hope, vowing never to return to it again. We shared his sentiments as we emerged guiltily from the unfriendly forest and felt the relief of seeing signposts to such reassuring-sounding places as Whitehall, Ben Lomond and Retirement. Our little adventure was over.

Indeed, our travels altogether were at an end. The coral reefs off the cays of San Felipe, the formidable walls of Santiago and

Campeche, the sweltering swamps of Tabasco, the alligator-infested *manigua* of southern Cuba, the sinuous waters of the Chagres river . . . all these and many other facets of the Caribbean we would not have experienced but for our perverse determination to re-enact Henry Morgan's exploits. Now – like him – we had completed the course.

'I feel,' said Caroline, after exchanging a sweaty farewell handshake with a much subdued Obadiah, 'as if I've earned the biggest daiquiri in the West Indies.'

She had, and she had it.

Select Bibliography

ACTS OF THE PRIVY COUNCIL OF ENGLAND: *Colonial Series* (Vol. I: 1613–1680 and Vol. II: 1680–1720)

BLACK, CLINTON V. *Our Archives* (Kingston, 1962)

BRYANT, ARTHUR *Samuel Pepys: The Years of Peril* (London, 1935)

BRYDALL, J. *Camera Regis* (London, 1676)

BUISSERET, DAVID *Historic Jamaica from the Air* (Barbados, 1969)

CALENDAR OF STATE PAPERS (COLONIAL): *America and West Indies* (1661–1688) *Addenda* (1658–1663)

CARLOS, RUBEN D. *220 Anos del periodo colonial en Panama* (Panama, 1969)

CRUIKSHANK, E. A. *The Life of Sir Henry Morgan* (Toronto, 1935)

DAMPIER, WILLIAM *A New Voyage Round the World* (London, 1697), *Voyage to Compeachy* (London 1729)

EARLE, PETER *The Sack of Panama* (London, 1981)

ESQUEMELING A. O. (JOHN) *The Buccaneers of America* (London, 1684)

EVELYN, JOHN *Diaries* (London, 1955)

FANSHAW PAPERS 1661–1665 (Borough Library, Dagenham)

FRASER, ANTONIA *King Charles II* (London, 1979)

GAGE, THOMAS *The English-American by sea and land, or a new survey of the West Indies* (London, 1648)

GREENE, GRAHAM *The Lawless Roads* (London, 1939)

HARING C. H. *The Buccaneers of the West Indies in the Seventeenth Century* (London, 1910)

HEMINGWAY, ERNEST *Islands in the Stream* (London, 1970)

JUAREZ, JUAN *Piratas y corsarios en Veracruz y Campeche* (Seville, 1972)

LABAT, JEAN-BAPTISTE *Nouveau voyage aux isles de l'Amérique* (Paris, 1722)

LEIGH FERMOR, PATRICK *The Traveller's Tree* (London, 1950)

LESLIE, CHARLES *New History of Jamaica* (London, 1740)

MCCULLOUGH, DAVID *The Path Between the Seas* (New York, 1977)

MASEFIELD, JOHN *The Spanish Main* (New York, 1906)

OGG, DAVID *England in the Reign of Charles II* (London, 1934)

PARRY, J. H. *The Spanish Seaborne Empire* (London, 1966)

PARRY, J. H. and SHERLOCK, P. M. *A Short History of the West Indies* (London, 1963)

PEPYS, SAMUEL *Diaries 1660–69* (London, 1848)

POPE, DUDLEY *Harry Morgan's Way* (London, 1977)

ROBERTS, W. ADOLPHE *Sir Henry Morgan: Buccaneer and Governor* (Kingston, 1952)

TESTA, BENITO REYES *Panamá la Vieja y Panamá la Nueva* (Panama, 1958)

THOMAS, HUGH *Cuba, or the Pursuit of Freedom* (London, 1971)

WARD, ESTELLE FRANCES *Christopher Monck, Duke of Albemarle* (London, 1915)

WINSTON, A. *No Purchase, No Pay* (Boston, 1969)

ZARAGOZA, JUSTO *Piraterías y agresiones de los ingleses* (Madrid, 1883)

Index

INSVLÆ AMERICANÆ IN OCE ANO SEPTENTRIONALI, cum Terris adiacentibus.

GOLFO DE MEXICO

MAR DEL ZVR

CVBA